365 DAYS OF VEGETARIAN RECIPES

EMMA KATIE

Check out more books by Emma Katie at:
www.amazon.com/author/emmakatie

CONTENTS

365 Days of Vegetarian Recipes

*1*NTRODUCTION

There are numerous vegetarian recipes, which are not only mouthwatering and delicious, but also make you stay healthy and help maintain a controlled balanced diet. Every human being needs vitamins, proteins and nutrients to maintain a good healthy body. Thus, I have written this book "365 days of Vegetarian Recipes", containing highly nutritious food recipes, which are easy to cook and serve. These are such recipes that your family and kids will love to eat on a daily basis.

There have been a lot of studies and researched that show why being vegetarian is a lot healthier. Here listed are a few advantages of following a vegetarian diet:

Lower body weight – Vegetarian foods do not have an excess amount of fates in them, especially as compared to the non-vegetarian food items. According to a research carried out by the Cancer Research UK, meat eaters gain more weight over a 5 year period as compared to the vegetarians.

Better cholesterol levels – We all know that eating red meat increases your cholesterol levels. A research done by the scientists at the University of Toronto and St. Michael's Hospital have found that eating particular plant foods decrease cholesterol and can be even used to treat patients with high cholesterol. Consuming a diet that consists of soy proteins, nuts (preferably almonds), margarine with plant sterols (a component present in leafy vegetables and vegetable oils) and high fiber foods like barley and oats, reduce the levels of 'bad' cholesterol in the body. This bad cholesterol often leads to the coronary artery getting clogged up.

Lower risk of cancer – Researchers working at the European Prospective Investigation into Cancer and Nutrition-Oxford (EPIC-Oxford) have discovered that vegetarians are at a lower risk of contracting cancer as compared to the meat eaters.

Extended life-span – As following a vegetarian diet plan protects you from a variety of ailments and diseases like diabetes, cardiovascular diseases, cancer, etc., every vegetarian's life expectancy increases when compared to the life expectancy of a non-vegetarian.

The dishes in this book can be prepared using very simple ingredients, which are easily available at both, your local supermarket as well as the farmer's market. The preparation is also very simple and unique, so that you can not only prepare the food perfectly, but also make the food taste better. Every single recipe that I have provided has been tested and can be made at home without using any difficult or highly technical methods. The recipes are written in a very easy language so that you can understand the exact way to prepare the delicious dishes without a lot of effort. The ingredients are also given with the exact quantities required, so that you get a perfect idea of the quantity of the dish you are going to prepare for your family members, viz. the number of servings you will be preparing. I assure you, you will find this book, "365 days of Vegetarian Recipes" very helpful and make you fall in love with cooking all over again! Some of the recipes that I have included in this book are:

Apricot and Blueberry Salsa
Oat Apple Crumble
Quinoa Side Dish
And many other recipes that are not only innovative but also extremely healthy.

365 Days of Vegetarian Recipes

Quinoa Side Dish

Quinoa is a highly healthy grain. It provides us with protection against hearing diseases, diabetes, hypertension, etc. Quinoa is rich in nutrition. Though named to be a side dish, this dish can be considered as a complete meal. It is easy to prepare and absolutely delicious!

Ingredients

18 ounces quinoa
36 oz. vegetable stock
4 red peppers
Lime juice as per taste

5 tablespoon olive oil
1 tablespoon freshly chopped cilantro
Salt and pepper to taste

Method

Toast the quinoa in a saucepan and add a drizzle of olive oil to. Add the vegetable stock to it and bring to a boil. Sprinkle salt and pepper. Stir well to avoid formation of clumps. Cook it for few minutes. Add the chopped red peppers, and freshly chopped cilantro. Spoon on to a plate and add a dash of lime juice to give it a tangy taste, acidic flavor. Serve hot. Enjoy!

Warm Corn Salad

This dish is a corn lover's heaven! It can be served as an appetizer, but also doubles up as a meal. The dish is easy to prepare and quite satiating.

Ingredients

1 teaspoon of butter
2 fresh corn, kernels are cut from the cob
½ diced red onion
1 tablespoon of chopped fresh parsley

pinch of salt to taste
freshly ground black pepper to sprinkle
1 tablespoon of chopped chives

Method

Take a skillet and melt the butter in it over medium-low heat. Add the fresh corn kernels and chopped red onion. Cook for about 5 minutes till they the red onion gets soft and tender. Mix in the parsley, and season with a pinch of salt and pepper. Garnish with chives and serve. Enjoy!

Sautéed Mange tout

This is a very easy dish and takes only 10 minutes to prepare. Mange tout is also known as sweet pea, which is crisp and sweet. It can be served raw, boiled or stir-fried. It is very healthy, tasty and adds a lot of texture to the dish.

Ingredients

3½ ounces mange tout
1 teaspoon toasted sesame seeds
1 tablespoon soy sauce

3 tablespoons of extra virgin olive oil
Slices of garlic (optional)
Salt and pepper to taste

Method

Wash the mange touts and remove the strings. Add them to a microwave safe bowl. Add the soy sauce, garlic (optional) and olive oil and cover the bowl completely, making it air tight. Microwave it till they become crisp and tender (this takes about 3 – 5 minutes). Transfer to a serving dish. Sprinkle some toasted sesame seeds, salt and pepper and this quick and easy dish is ready to serve. Enjoy!

Roasted Cauliflower with Parmesan

Cauliflowers are extremely healthy and tasty. Its delicious flavor doubles with a touch of Parmesan and garlic. The dish is roasted and is extremely satiating.

Ingredients

1 large cauliflower, cut into florets
4 tablespoons of extra virgin olive oil
1 cup grated Parmesan cheese

Salt to taste
Freshly ground black pepper to taste
2½ tablespoons of minced garlic

Method

Preheat the oven to 400 degrees F. Take a casserole dish and grease it well with some cooking spray. Take a re-sealable bag and add the olive oil, minced garlic and cauliflower florets to it and shake it well, until the olive oil coats the florets completely. Pour the contents of the re-sealable bag into the greased casserole dish. Sprinkle salt and pepper for seasoning. Bake in the preheated oven for 20-25 minutes. Add the grated Parmesan cheese to the cauliflower florets and broil it for a few more minutes. Cook until the cauliflower gets a hint of brown color to it. Serve hot. Enjoy!

Buttery Spinach

Usually kids cringe at the sight of spinach, but spinach is a very healthy and nutrient rich vegetable. Spinach is low in fat and high in important nutrients, such as iron and vitamins, such as vitamin A. This dish is one of the easiest and fastest to cook side dish.

Ingredients

2 packets of spinach (frozen)
½ cup butter

Salt to taste
Pinch of garlic powder to taste

Method

Take the packaged frozen spinach in a bowl. Rinse it well with cold water for several minutes. Then allow it to drain completely. Once drained, cut into long strips. Heat a sauce pan over medium-low heat. Add the butter and then the chopped spinach. Add a bit more butter if you wish to have a more buttery flavor. Cook till the spinach starts to wilt around the edges. Remove onto a serving plate and sprinkle the garlic powder and salt to taste, just before serving. Serve it immediately. Enjoy!

PARMESAN ASPARAGUS

Asparagus is very nutritious and delicious. Moreover, the addition of parmesan cheese makes the dish even more delicious. You can serve this dish as an appetizer or a side dish.

Ingredients

1 pound asparagus spears
1 cup shredded Parmesan cheese
Freshly ground black pepper to season

1½ tablespoons of extra virgin olive oil
1 teaspoon Balsamic Vinegar

Method

Firstly, preheat the oven to 400 degrees F. Wash the asparagus thoroughly and arrange on a baking sheet. Drizzle the olive oil and toss well until the olive oil uniformly coats the asparagus. Top the asparagus with the shredded Parmesan cheese. Sprinkle some black pepper. Now, pop the baking sheet into the preheated oven and bake for about 15 minutes. When the asparagus turns crisp and tender and cheese has completely melted, remove from the baking sheet on to a serving plate. Sprinkle the Balsamic vinegar and serve hot. Enjoy!

ROASTED BRUSSELS SPROUTS

Roasted Brussels sprouts taste absolutely delicious and are really easy to prepare. You can serve this dish as a side dish or even as a main dish, as this dish is quite filling.

Ingredients

2 pounds of Brussels sprouts, ends are trimmed and yellow leaves discarded
3 tablespoons of extra virgin olive oil

A pinch of salt to taste
Sprinkle freshly ground black pepper for taste

Method

Firstly, preheat the oven to 400 degrees F. Wash the sprouts thoroughly. In a re-sealable bag, add the Brussels sprouts, olive oil and a pinch of salt and freshly ground black pepper in it. Seal the bag and shake well until the olive oil coats the sprouts. Spread the Brussels sprouts on a greased baking tray in a single layer and pop into the preheated oven. Bake for about 35 to 40 minutes, continuously turning the Brussels sprouts at an interval of 6 minutes. Keep a check of the heat, so that they don't burn up. When the Brussels sprouts get a dark brown to blackish hue know that they are ready to serve. Taste and season accordingly. Serve immediately. Enjoy!

Honey Roasted Red Potatoes

This is simple and quick recipe to prepare. You can serve it as a side dish or have it as a snack.

Ingredients

A pound of quartered red potatoes
One finely diced onion
2 tablespoons of melted butter
1 tablespoon of honey

A teaspoon of dry mustard
a pinch salt to taste
1 pinch of freshly ground black pepper

Method

Firstly, preheat the oven to 325 degrees F. Coat a baking dish with nonstick cooking spray. Arrange potatoes in a single layer on the prepared baking dish, and top them with the onion. In a bowl, mix melted butter, honey, mustard, pinch of salt and pepper. Brush this mix on the potatoes and onion. Bake till the potatoes are tender. Serve hot. Enjoy!

Fried Kale

Kale is a very healthy vegetable and is an excellent source of antioxidants. Moreover, when tossed with garlic the kale become even tastier to consume. This dish can be served as a side dish.

Ingredients

A bunch of kale
4-5 minced garlic cloves

Generous drizzle of olive oil
Pinch of salt and pepper to taste

Method

Take fresh kale leaves and wash well. Remove the stems and tear the leaves into bite sized pieces. Heat a pot over medium-high heat and drizzle some olive oil in it. Add the minced garlic into the oil and cook until the garlic is soft. Add the pieces of kale leaves and continue to stir until the leaves start to wilt. It takes about 5 to 6 minutes for leaves to turn into bright green. Serve immediately. Enjoy!

Asparagus with Balsamic Butter Sauce

Asparagus is very nutritious and yummy. Moreover, when served with the Balsamic butter sauce the asparagus tastes even more mouthwateringly delicious. You can serve the dish as an appetizer or a side dish.

Ingredients

A bunch of trimmed fresh asparagus
Cooking spray to grease
Pinch of salt
Pepper to taste

2 tablespoons butter
1 tablespoon of soy sauce
Little drizzle of balsamic vinegar

Method

Firstly, preheat the oven to 400 degrees F. Wash the asparagus and arrange the asparagus on a baking sheet. Spray with cooking spray. Season with salt and pepper. Bake for about 12 minutes in the preheated oven till the asparagus are tender. Melt about 2 tablespoons of butter over medium heat or put in a microwave safe bowl and microwave for about 30 seconds. Once the butter is liquefied stir in a drizzle of soy sauce and balsamic vinegar. Pour this over the baked asparagus and serve immediately. Enjoy!

PARMESAN CAULIFLOWER

Cauliflower is one of the most popularly consumed vegetables. Baked cauliflower is extremely delicious as well extremely healthy to eat.

Ingredients

1 whole fresh Cauliflower
1 stick of butter
1½ tablespoons of Mayonnaise

1 teaspoon of mustard (prepared)
1 cup grated parmesan cheese
Oregano to taste

Method

Firstly, steam the whole cauliflower and place it on a pie plate. Take a mixing bowl and mix Mayonnaise and the prepared mustard. Spread this mixture on the steamed cauliflower. Top it up with the grated Parmesan cheese. Pop it into an oven which was preheated to 400 degrees F. Bake for about 30 minutes, till the cheese melts and top with a pinch of oregano and serve immediately. Enjoy!

CANDIED CARROTS

Carrots are very healthy and nutrition rich. The candied carrots can be served as a dish by themselves or can be added to other vegetables to make a nutritious salad..

Ingredients

5 ounces fresh carrots, cut into 2 inch pieces
2 tablespoons of diced butter

1 tablespoon packed brown sugar
1 pinch of salt to taste
1 pinch of freshly ground black pepper

Method

Boil the carrots in a pot of salted water. Reduce heat and let it simmer. Cook for about 25 to 35 minutes. Do not overcook the carrots; they should be tender, yet firm. Drain the carrots. Reduce the heat to its lowest and return the carrots to the pan. Now, stir in diced butter, brown sugar, pinch of salt and pepper. Cook for about 4 to 6 minutes, until they get caramelized. Serve them hot. Enjoy!

GRILLED VEGETABLES

This dish makes the fresh vegetables more tempting and tasty. This dish can be served as a meal or a snack. This dish is highly nutritious and low in fat.

Ingredients

1 cup summer squash, cut into juliennes
1 cup fresh zucchini, cut into juliennes
1 cup florets of cauliflower
1 cup asparagus spears
1cup bell peppers, diced

1 cup onions. diced
Extra virgin olive oil
Pinch of salt
Pepper to taste

Method

Take all the fresh vegetables and wash them thoroughly with cold water before chopping them. Preheat the oven grill. Place the vegetables in a large mixing bowl. Drizzle some olive oil, pinch of salt and pepper. Toss gently so that the vegetables get uniformly coated. Now arrange them on grill sprayed with some cooking spray. Grill them for about half an hour till they are tender. Enjoy!

BROCCOLI IN BUTTER SAUCE

This dish is very tasty and quickly prepared. This broccoli dish can be consumed any time, in the form of a side dish or main dish. It is very filling as well.

Ingredients

A Fresh Broccoli, cut into florets
3 tablespoons butter
3 Minced garlic cloves

3 tablespoons of lime juice
Salt to taste
Pinch of pepper

Method

Firstly, steam the broccoli. Boil it till it is tender and drain. Melt the butter in a saucepan over a medium heat and sauté minced garlic. Now, remove the saucepan from the heat and add the lemon juice. Stir well. Then pour this mixture onto the steamed broccoli. Sprinkle some salt and black pepper to taste. Serve this delicious dish hot within 15-20 minutes of preparing it for maximum taste. Enjoy!

HONEYED PEANUTS

This is a very easy to prepare snack or you can have a handful of them for breakfast to add some crunch to your meals. Nuts are very healthy and are tasty to eat.

Ingredients

1 cup peanuts
Drizzle of Canola oil

5 tablespoons Honey
Pinch of cinnamon

Method

Take a skillet and heat it over medium heat and grease it with canola oil. Now, add the peanuts to the skillet and keep them stirring them around till they get toasted and a nutty aroma fills the kitchen. Sprinkle cinnamon and honey to the pan. Continue cooking for about 3 to 4 minutes till the honey becomes sticky and starts caramelizing. Remove from heat and place the peanuts on wax paper and let them cool a bit. Break apart and cool. Serve warm and store the leftover peanuts in an air tight container away from direct sunlight. Enjoy!

MICROWAVE POTATO CHIPS

This is very easy to cook and a very popular recipe. People love to have them as a snack or as a side along with a sandwich. As these potato chips are not fried, they are a much healthier alternative to the regular fat ridden potato chips.

Ingredients

4-5 potatoes (large)
Garlic powder to taste
Cayenne pepper to taste

Dried dill weed to taste
Salt for seasoning
Oil (Vegetable oil is preferred)

Method

Take the potatoes, wash them well and peel the skin. Cut them in thin slices. Place the potato slices in a bowl, along with salt and cover with water and let them sit for about 10-12 minutes. Drain and arrange the potato slices on a microwave safe tray, which has already been greased with some vegetable oil. Now sprinkle Cayenne pepper, garlic powder and dried dill weed. Sprinkle a bit of oil over the potato chips and microwave for 5-6 minutes. Enjoy!

BAKED EGGPLANT

This is a very simple and tasty dish. You can make it in flat 30 minutes. You can serve it as appetizer or a side dish.

Ingredients

1 large eggplant
⅓rd cup of Mayonnaise
1 cup breadcrumbs
½ cup of grated Parmesan
1 large onion, minced
Dried Italian seasoning to sprinkle
Cooking spray

Method

Preheat the oven to 400 degrees F. Wash and cut the eggplant into ½ inch thick slices. Arrange these slices on a baking sheet which has been sprayed with cooking spray. In a separate bowl, mix together the mayonnaise and minced onion and spread them over the sliced eggplants. In another bowl, mix breadcrumbs, Parmesan and Italian seasoning and drown the eggplants in this mixture and put them back to the sheet. Bake in the preheated oven for about 10-12 minutes or until the eggplant is firm yet tender to touch. Serve hot. Enjoy!

SPINACH STRAWBERRY SALAD

Spinach and strawberry may seem like an odd combination, but I assure you, when they are combined together they taste delicious and will appeal to the fussiest of eaters!

Ingredients

1 packet fresh spinach, torn apart into bite sized pieces
1 packet fresh strawberries, cut into quarters
Toasted pecans

1 cup Red wine vinegar, raspberry flavor
½ cup sugar
1 teaspoon dry mustard
Drizzle of vegetable oil
2 teaspoons of poppy seeds

Method

Take a bowl and combine red wine raspberry vinegar, sugar, dried mustard, poppy seeds and drizzle of vegetable oil. Mix them well and your dressing is ready. Now, take a big salad mixing bowl and add the fresh spinach. Drizzle the dressing and start tossing, in order to ensure uniform coating. Add the fresh strawberries to the bowl. Top with some chopped toasted pecans. Serve the salad immediately. Enjoy!

GLAZED CARROTS

This is a very tasty and healthy dish. It hardly takes time to prepare. It is refreshing as well as very satiating.

Ingredients

1 pound fresh carrots
1 and a half stick of butter
Sugar to taste
Salt to taste

6-7 tablespoons of maple syrup
3 tablespoons brown sugar
Chopped fresh parsley

Method

Heat a large pot with water in it. Cut the carrots into slices horizontally and add them to the pot along with about half stick of the butter, sugar and salt. Boil and then simmer till the carrots become tender. Drain and keep aside. Heat a skillet over medium heat melt rest of the butter in it. Add the maple syrup and brown sugar to it. Keep on stirring till the sugar dissolves. Add the carrots and cook for another 5-6 minutes. Sprinkle salt, pepper and chopped parsley over it. Enjoy!

HOMEMADE CRANBERRY SAUCE

This is an extremely delicious sauce that invokes a lot of holiday spirit. This sauce is loved by all, especially the kids. The sauce takes about 5 to 10 minutes to prepare and you can store it in a refrigerator for a period of time.

Ingredients

12 ounces of fresh juicy cranberries
1 cup sugar or artificial sweetener

1 cup orange juice (you may use 1 cup of plain water)

Method

Take a big bowl, fill it with water and rinse the fresh cranberries very well. Drain. Add 1 cup of sugar or artificial sweetener and 1 cup of water or orange juice to the cranberries. Mix them thoroughly and transfer them to a saucepan and bring the mix to a boil. Once bubbling, reduce the heat and simmer for a while. Remove from the heat when the sauce is thick and cool to room temperature. Pour the sauce into an airtight container and chill in the refrigerator for at least 8 hours before serving. Enjoy!

SPICY ONION RINGS

Onions are one of the most important and commonly used vegetables in the world. When they are fried they become even tastier. This is fried dish can be served as a side with burgers or sandwiches or eaten alone.

Ingredients

1 cup flour
Warm or cold water, as needed
Salt to taste
Paprika to make it spicy, to taste

4 large onions
Vegetable or extra virgin olive oil, for frying

Method

Firstly, take 1 cup of flour (self-rising) and mix it with warm or cold water until you attain a uniformly runny consistency. Now, add paprika to make it spicy and salt according to your taste.
Cut the fresh onions into rings and drench the rings into the mixture until evenly coated. Now, deep fry the onion rings till they become crispy and crunchy. Serve them hot and delicious. Enjoy!

CHEESY DIP RICE

This dish is very tasty and everyone loves it. This is an easy recipe that can be prepared quickly.

Ingredients

A handful of salad rocket
1 cup rice

Extra virgin olive oil
1 container tortilla cheese dip

Water, as needed
Hot vegetable stock, as needed

Salt and pepper to taste
Oregano (if you wish)

Method

First, steam the rice in a mixture of the water and vegetable stock (mixed in a 1:1 ratio). Drain it. Add drizzle of extra virgin olive oil, tortilla cheese dip to the cooked rice and mix them thoroughly. Add a handful of salad rocket. Again mix thoroughly. You can serve this dish steaming hot. You may refrigerate this prepared dish and serve it cold. The dish tastes best when it is served cold. Enjoy!

BAKED BUTTERNUT SQUASH FRIES

This is a very easy and flavorsome dish. You can serve it as an appetizer or as a side dish or even as a snack..

Ingredients

1 fresh butternut squash
Drizzle of extra virgin olive oil

Garlic salt to season
Freshly ground black pepper to taste

Method

Wash the butternut squash, peel off the skin and cut it into ½ inch slices. Then preheat the oven to 400 degrees F. Arrange the butternut squash slices in a single layer in a greased baking tray. Drizzle extra virgin olive oil and season with a pinch of garlic salt and freshly ground black pepper. Pop into the preheated oven and bake till they are crispy and crunchy. Serve the fries hot with sprinkle of salt. Enjoy!

VEGETABLE COUS COUS

This is a very filling dish which you can serve during your meals. This is very easy to prepare and does not require any fancy ingredients or equipment's.

Ingredients

1 cup Couscous
½ cup mushrooms (any type)
½ cup peeled tomatoes, diced
½ cup sweet corn kernels

½ cup chickpeas
Salt to taste
Black pepper to taste

Method

Fill a pot with water and add the couscous and bring it to a boil. When the couscous is cooked, drain the water. The cooking process should take about 5 to 6 minutes. Meanwhile, chop the mushrooms and place in a microwaveable bowl. Then add the tomatoes, chickpeas and the sweet corn to the mushrooms. Place this in the microwave for about 2 to 3 minutes. Now add this to the cooked couscous. Mix well and season with salt and pepper. Serve hot. Enjoy!

BREAD PIZZA

Making a pizza is a very arduous affair and it may seem easier to just order in! But, here we present you with a quick and easy recipe to prepare a delicious and healthy pizza hat your children will relish!

Ingredients

12 bread slices
½ cup tomato sauce
4 tablespoons melted butter
½ cup mozzarella cheese, grated
2 onions

2 tomatoes
2 capsicums
2 tablespoons of olive oil
A pinch of oregano
Salt and pepper to taste

Method

M Wash the onions, tomatoes and capsicums and dice uniformly. Put them in a bowl and add the olive oil, pinch of oregano, salt and pepper and mix well. Place the bowl in the freezer for about 5 minutes. You can store this mix in the fridge for at least 3 days. Pour the tomato sauce in a bowl and mix in the butter. Spread it on slice of bread. Spread a layer of the mozzarella, then the vegetable mix and top it with the mozzarella and heat in the microwave till the cheese melts. Serve immediately.
Enjoy

PEANUT RICE

This is a very simple and scrumptious dish. It can be prepared within half an hour, ideal for when you are on a time crunch! You can serve it as a main dish, as it is quite satiating.

Ingredients

7-8 cups of rice
2 large onions, finely chopped
1 cup soy sauce
2½ tubs of creamy peanut butter

1 garlic clove, finely chopped
4 chilies
Salt to taste
Pepper to taste

Method

Take a pot with water and add the rice to. Bring it to boil and simmer until the rice is cooked. Keep aside. Take a skillet and stir fry the garlic, chilies and onions until soft. Pour the soy sauce and peanut butter to the rice and mix well. Add the contents in the skillet into the rice and peanut butter mix and heat on a low heat for 6-12 minutes, continuously stirring it. Serve hot. Enjoy!

DELIGHTFUL BEANS

Beans are some of the most healthy and nutritious foods. For vegetarians, beans like soya beans are extremely important as they are the main source of proteins. It is very easy to prepare this dish and make sure you are receiving your daily dose of proteins.

Ingredients

1 can of beans (preferably soya beans)	1 cube of vegetable stock
1 clove of garlic, finely chopped	1 fresh onion, chopped
2 tomatoes, peeled and chopped	Drizzle of Vegetable oil

Method

Drizzle a bit of vegetable oil in a medium sized skillet over medium heat. Add the onions and garlic to the skillet and sauté until tender. Fill a pot with some water and heat until gently simmering. Add in the vegetable stock cube and mix well. Pour the stock into the skillet with the onions and garlic and add the tomatoes and beans to it. Cook on a medium flame, for about 10 minutes or until the beans are tender. Serve hot. Enjoy!

FRIED ONION AND CABBAGE

Both these vegetables are very nutritious and delicious as well. You can make so many recipes with them. This recipe makes a tasty and nutritious snack.

Ingredients

1 large potato	Salt to taste
1 large red onion	Freshly ground black pepper to taste
1 head of cabbage	Extra virgin olive oil for sautéing

Method

Firstly, steam the cabbage and keep it aside. Now, finely dice the onion and fry in a sauce pan with some extra virgin olive oil. Finely grate the potato. As the chopped onion begins to turn brown, add the grated potato to it and mix well. Add the cooked cabbage to the onions and potatoes and mix well .Sprinkle some black pepper and salt according to your taste and serve them hot and crispy. Enjoy!

SPINACH SAUTÉ

Spinach is a very rich source of nutrition. Not only healthy, but it is tasty as well. This dish is easy to prepare and quite satiating.

Ingredients

2 tablespoons of butter	Pinch of salt
2 garlic cloves, finely chopped	Sprinkle freshly ground black pepper
10 ounce of spinach (fresh)	Juice of ½ lemon

Method

Melt the butter in a sauce pan over medium heat. Add the garlic and stir till it turns is golden brown. Be careful so that the garlic does not burn. Turn to high and add the fresh spinach, flipping every minute, till they start to wilt around the edges. Take the sauce pan off the heat. Season with salt and pepper and add in the lemon juice. Toss well and serve immediately. Enjoy!

Pumpkin Pancakes

Don't limit your family's pumpkin intake just to Halloween. Kick start your day with this nutritious and delicious dish!

Ingredients

2 cups of coconut flour
1 teaspoon baking powder
A pinch of salt
A pinch of cinnamon
1 cup coconut milk

4 tablespoons melted butter
4 tablespoons maple syrup
Few drops of vanilla extract
Pinch of pie spice
1 cup pumpkin puree

Method

Mix the flour, baking powder, pinch of salt, cinnamon and pie spice in a bowl and whisk together. In another bowl combine the coconut milk, pumpkin puree, butter, vanilla extract and maple syrup. Pour this mixture into the dry ingredients and fold in a clockwise motion. Melt some butter on a griddle and pour this batter onto the griddle in circular motions. Cook on both sides until evenly browned. Enjoy!

Toasted Quinoa Tabbouleh

Ingredients

1½ cups of quinoa
1 ¾ teaspoon sea salt, divided
⅓ cup of olive oil
¾ cup lemon juice
2 cloves of garlic
½ teaspoon of ground black pepper

2 cups diced tomatoes
1½ cups parsley
3 unpeeled Persian cucumbers
1 cup green onions
½ cup mint leaves

Method

Rinse quinoa in a strainer under water. Add to a large skillet and heat till golden and fragrant, stirring constantly. Bring water to boil in a saucepan. Add salt (¼ teaspoons) and then quinoa. Reduce heat and boil again and then simmer for 20 minutes, till the quinoa is soft and all the liquid has been absorbed. Fluff it using fork and place in a bowl. Let it cool. Whisk lemon juice, oil, pepper and garlic with the remaining salt in a bowl. Stir well with tomatoes, cucumbers, parsley, mint leaves and green onions into quinoa. Pour marinade over it and toss till well-coated. Refrigerate to serve chill. Enjoy!

Bell Pepper, Olive and Arugula Salsa

This Mediterranean inspired salsa brings out delicious flavor and smell. For better results, prepare the recipe just before serving for crunchy taste; serve while warm at room temperature.

Ingredients

1½ teaspoons olive oil
1 teaspoons fennel seeds
2 small bell peppers (1 yellow and 1 red)

16 Kalamata olives, quartered
½ cup packed baby arugula, chopped

Method

Take large nonstick pan and heat oil with fennel seeds added, over medium heat. Stir occasionally. Add bell peppers and sauté for about 4 minutes until peppers begin to get tender. Remove the oil and bell peppers into medium sized bowl and mix olives in it. Let it stand for 2 minutes after seasoning with pepper and salt. Let the flavors infuse properly. Combine with arugula and toss till arugula lightly wilted. Enjoy!

SWEET-AND-SOUR BAKED TOFU

It can be easily served as a delicious breakfast.

Ingredients

1½ tablespoons soy sauce
1½ tablespoons lime juice
1 tablespoons red chili sauce
½ tablespoons olive oil
½ teaspoons brown sugar
14oz (6 slices) tofu

2 tablespoons roasted peanuts
2 pcs green onions
1 tablespoons ginger
1½ cups shredded red cabbage
2 pc (4" each) Ciabatta rolls, halved lengthwise

Method

Preheat oil to 400 degrees F. Grease a baking dish with some cooking spray. Whisk together the sugar, soy sauce, chili sauce, lime juice and oil in a bowl. Add tofu slices and marinate for 10 minutes, flipping twice. Transfer tofu to the baking dish and sprinkle peanuts, onion and ginger over it. Bake until brown. Let it cool. Toss cabbage with left over marinade. Discard excess of bread from rolls' center. Place 3 slices of tofu on bottom half and garnish with cabbage. Close sandwich and store in refrigerator. Enjoy!

PINEAPPLE, CUCUMBER AND AVOCADO SALSA

This crunchy, spicy and creamy salsa has a sweet flavor and serves as a filling appetizer on its own. The dish is quite healthy and can be easily served at any point of time.

Ingredients

1⅓ cups cucumber
½ pc pineapple, peeled, diced and cored
¼ cup green onions, sliced
3-4 teaspoons red jalapeno chili, chopped
8oz avocado, peeled, diced and deseeded

Method

Stir the pineapple, green onions, cucumber and chili together in a bowl. Squeeze the pineapple slices using garlic press, extracting about ¼ cup of juice. Stir juice into salsa and fold in the avocado. Season with pepper and salt if required and let it set for about 5 minutes before you serve. The recipe makes about 3 cups of the appetizer. Enjoy!

Black-Eyed Pea Chili

Ingredients

½ lb. black-eyed peas
2 tablespoons coconut oil
1 cup onion
1 cup green bell pepper
2 teaspoons garlic cloves

1 can (15 oz.) fire-roasted tomatoes
2 tablespoons tomato puree
1 tablespoon chili powder
1 cup vegetable broth
½ cup green onions

Method

Soak the black-eyed peas in water for 8 hrs. Rinse well. Put the setting to 'sauté' and preheat rice cooker for 2-3 minutes. Add oil and heat. Add onion and sauté. Combine bell pepper and garlic and sauté again for 4 minutes until softened. Stir in the tomato puree, tomatoes and chili powder. Simmer for few minutes. Adjust setting to 'slow cook' and pour in black-eyed peas and vegetable broth. Cook for 5 hours till the peas are tender. Add pepper and salt and garnish with green onions. Enjoy!

Japanese Noodle Soup

Ingredients

6 cloves of garlic
4 pieces of green onions
2 pcs (5inch each) Kombu
7 small coins of ginger
¼ cup Tamari sauce
3 tablespoons Mirin
2 teaspoons Sugar

2 cups Shiitake mushrooms
3 pc carrots
4 cups rice noodles, cooked
2 cups snow peas
4 teaspoons sesame oil
2 teaspoons sesame seeds

Method

Chop the garlic cloves. Put in cooker. Add white parts of green onions along with ginger and Kombu to cooker. Chop green onions and set aside. Add mirin, tamari, water and sugar to the cooker and cook for 6 hours. Strain and remove solid parts and return liquid back to cooker. Add carrots and mushrooms and cook for 1 hour until vegetables tender. Split noodles in 4 bowls and top with peas. Pour broth and garnish with sesame oil, onions and seeds. Enjoy!

CURRIED CHEESE AND PEACH PANINI

Ingredients

2 cups cottage cheese 2cups
1 teaspoon curry powder
½ teaspoon ginger
¼ teaspoon lime zest
¼ cup celery, chopped

2 tablespoons green onion, chopped
10 oz. sour dough baguette
½ cup mango chutney
1 large peach, sliced
8 tablespoons almonds, sliced

Method

Stir cheese, ginger, curry powder and lime zest in a bowl. Fold in the onions and celery. Set aside. Divide baguette lengths with one side attached. Discard excess bread for filling space. Spread 2 tablespoons chutney and fill with ½ cheese mixture, 2 tablespoons almonds and 4 peach slices. Use cooking spray for spraying Panini tops and coat skillet with cooking spray and put on medium heat. Add Panini and cook for 3 minutes, placing 2 cans weight on it. Flip Panini once and replace weight and cook for 2 more minutes until almost crisp. Enjoy!

BAKED POTATO PIZZA

This yummy and delicious pizza would surely delight your guests and will make your kids go-crazy for it. Par-baked pizza crust can be used for two days while kept in fridge or for months if kept in freezer.

Ingredients

3 tablespoons olive oil
1 gluten-free pizza crust, par-baked
1 garlic clove, minced
1 baked potato, sliced

½ cup raw broccoli florets
⅔ cup cheddar cheese, shredded
⅓ cup sour cream
Chives ¼ cup, chopped

Method

Preheat oven to 425 degrees F. Grease 2 tablespoons oil over par-baked pizza crust. Put the garlic, broccoli florets and sliced potato as toppings. Drizzle 1 tablespoon olive oil and add sour cream and cheddar cheese in dollops. Bake until cheese bubbling, for around 7 minutes. Remove and then sprinkle chives over it. Serve hot. Enjoy!

DARK CHOCOLATE AND BANANA PANINI

Bananas are the healthiest of all the diet food for their calcium enriched features. When combined with chocolate it gives a rare taste of Panini. So have some bites of this wonderful recipe.

Ingredients

2 bananas, large in size and sliced

8 slices of sourdough bread or sprouted wheat

4 oz. of dark chocolate, bittersweet and chopped
4 teaspoons of honey

Method

Place the banana slices on 4 slices of bread. Sprinkle 3 tablespoons of chocolate on each of the slices. Add 1 teaspoons of honey. Now, cover with the remaining pieces of bread. Take Panini maker and preheat. Coat the maker with butter flavored cooking spray. Cook the Panini from both the sides for 3-4 minutes. Allow it to cool for 5 minutes and then serve. Enjoy!

MEDITERRANEAN VEGGIE BURGERS

Vegetables are absolutely essential for a good health, but most children usually cringe at the sight of them! Here's a way to cleverly incorporate veggies into their meal quite effortlessly and in a way that they will relish them!

Ingredients

4 oz. of rigatoni
7 oz. of vegetable broth, low sodium
½ cup of red quinoa
1½ teaspoon of olive oil
¾ cup of onion, chopped
9 cloves of garlic, finely chopped
1½ cups of white beans, cooked
½ cup of broccoli, steamed

¼ cup and 2 tablespoons of green cabbage, shredded finely
3 tablespoons of red bell pepper, finely chopped
2 tablespoons of tomato sauce
6 Kalama olives, sliced
2 tomatoes, oil-packed and sun dried, drained and chopped finely
2 tablespoons of canola oil

Method

Boil rigatoni in pot of salted water for 19 minutes or until tender. Drain and keep aside 1½ cups tight rigatoni. Boil broth and quinoa in a saucepan. Cook for 13 minutes on low heat. Drain. In a small pan, heat oil on medium flame. Add onion and cook for 1 minute. Now, add garlic and cook for another 1 minute. In a processor, process rigatoni and beans until smooth. Pour the batter into a bowl and add quinoa, broccoli, bell pepper, olives, cabbage, tomatoes, and the onion-garlic mixture and combine. Mash the mixture and make patties and brush them with oil. Heat the grill and brush with oil. Place the patties on the grill and cook for 6-7 minutes. Turn the sides and cook again. Serve hot. Enjoy!

BLUE CHEESE RADICCHIO AND FIG SANDWICHES

Sandwiches are said to be healthy and are the favorite food of all ages. Mix of cheese, figs and radicchio is awesome to prepare such healthy and tasty sandwiches.

Ingredients

3 oz. of blue cheese, crumbled

3 oz. of cream cheese, reduced-fat

8 slices of whole-grain bread, sprouted
8 teaspoons of butter, melted and trans-fat free

4 tablespoons of jam, fig
1 cup of radicchio, sliced thinly

Method

Mash both the cheese together in a mixing bowl. Set aside few chunks of blue cheese. Apply butter on the 4 slices of bread. Apply some butter on the baking sheet too. Spread 1 tablespoon jam and ¼ cup of radicchio on each slice of bread. Cover the remaining 4 slices with the cheese mixture and place them on top of the radicchio. Now apply the remaining butter on the top of the slices. Take large skillet and heat it on medium heat. Now, cook both the sides of the sandwiches for 3 to 4 minutes until crisp and brown. Serve hot. Enjoy!

HOMEMADE TOMATO SOUP

This is the easiest and tastiest tomato soup, apt for a cold winter day.

Ingredients

2 tablespoons of olive oil
1 onion, medium sized, chopped
1 tablespoon of tomato paste
2 cloves of garlic, minced
1 teaspoon of sugar

1 can (12 oz.) tomatoes, diced
1 vegetable cube, optional
2 teaspoons of vinegar, balsamic
½ teaspoon of thyme, dried

Method

Take a medium sized saucepan and place it on medium heat. Add the chopped onions and sauté for 5 minutes. Add tomato paste, sugar and garlic and cook for 1 minute. Now combine diced tomatoes, vinegar, vegetable cube (if required), thyme and 4 cups of water and bring to a boil. Simmer the soup for 15 minutes. Now remove the saucepan from heat and blend it in a blender. Add pepper and salt if desired. Serve hot. Enjoy!

STIR-FRIED BROCCOLI FLORETS, STEMS AND LEAVES

Broccoli is excellent in taste and wonderful for vegetable diet plan.

Ingredients

1 broccoli, large head
1 navel orange, large sized and washed
2 tablespoons of lemon juice
1 tablespoon of soy sauce
1 tablespoon of brown sugar
1 tablespoon of fresh ginger julienned, and 2 teaspoons of minced, divided
1 teaspoon of cornstarch

3 tablespoons of vegetable oil
2 shallots, large sized, peeled and sliced thinly
1 large garlic clove, peeled and sliced thinly
½ teaspoon of salt

Method

Remove the leaves of broccoli and slice them thinly. Remove the florets and trim them into 1-2 inch florets. Cut the broccoli stalk in thin slices. Peel the zest from orange in about 6-7 long and ½ an inch wide strips. Pile the strips and slice thinly to julienne . Stir 3 tablespoons of orange juice and lemon juice along with soy sauce, minced ginger, brown sugar and cornstarch in a small bowl. Keep aside. Place a wok on medium heat and add broccoli leaves, orange zest julienned, ginger julienned, garlic and shallots. Fry for 2 minutes and remove in a plate. Add the other 1 tablespoon of oil to a wok and heat over medium heat. Add florets and stalks and add salt for seasoning. Combine juice mixture. Allow to cool and then toss with the leaves. Enjoy!

TANGY SWEET PIZZA

Pizz1 can be made in innumerable ways. There are lots of toppings to be prepared and presented. This sweet and tangy combination is definitely going to make your taste buds go crazy, along with being extremely healthy for your body too.

Ingredients

¼ cup of tomato pesto, sun-dried
1 Gluten-Free Pizza Crust, par-baked
1½ cups of sweet potatoes, cooked and sliced

½ cup of red onion, sliced thinly
⅔ cup of feta cheese, crumbled
2 cups of baby arugula

Method

Brush the tomato pesto over the Pizza Crust. Add the toppings of red onions, sweet potatoes and feta cheese. Set the oven at 425 degrees F and bake the pizza for 5-7 minutes. Let the cheese melt and toppings turn brown. Remove the pizza from pan and serve after topping the pizza with the baby arugula. Enjoy!

FRESH CORN AND TOMATILLO SALSA

The combination of corn and tomatillo tastes absolutely scrumptious and makes a delectable accompaniment with a variety of tacos and chips.

Ingredients

1½ cups of fresh, husked tomatillos, chopped
1½ cups of corn kernels, fresh
6 tablespoons of cilantro, chopped

1 tablespoon of jalapeno chili along with seeds, chopped
1 tablespoon of fresh lime juice

Method

Take the tomatillos in a small bowl and microwave on high power for 2 minutes till they turn saucy. Scatter the sauce on a pie dish. Shift to freezer for quick cooling. Place a nonstick skillet over medium heat and coat it with cooking spray. Now, add corn and stir for 2 minutes. Allow it to cool and shift to freezer for fast cooling. Now mix jalapeno, lemon juice and cilantro in a bowl. Add corn and tomato sauce to it. Taste and season accordingly. Enjoy!

HUMMUS PIE

This is a simple recipe of pizza to prepare. Hummus and other spices are extremely flavorful. Roasted red peppers and onions add spice to this recipe. Go on, prepare this for your children and watch as they squeal in joy at the amazingness of this dish. It will make both, their holiday and health enjoyable.

Ingredients

1¼ cups of hummus
1 Gluten Free Pizza Crust, par baked
½ cup of red peppers, roasted and chopped

⅓ cup of red onion, chopped
1 teaspoon of sumac, ground
Cilantro for garnishing

Method

Spread the hummus over the pizza crust. Add toppings of roasted red peppers, ground sumac and red onion. Bake the pizza in a preheated oven at 425 degrees F for 5-7 minutes. Garnish with the cilantro. Serve hot. Enjoy!

RED CURRY VEGETABLE SOUP

Soup is healthier and tastier than most other diet recipes, thanks to the variety of ingredients you add to it and its satiating properties.

Ingredients

1 tablespoon of canola oil
12 oz. of cauliflower, cut into florets of 1 inch
4 green onions, large sized and sliced thinly, separating the green and white parts
2 tablespoons of Thai red curry paste

4 cups of vegetable broth, low sodium
1 can (15-oz.) of tomatoes, diced and juiced
¾ cup of coconut milk, light
6 oz. of green beans, cut into pieces
1 tablespoon of lime juice

Method

Put a large saucepan on medium heat and add oil. Add cauliflower and white parts of the green onion and stir for 5 minutes. Stir in the curry paste and mix for 1 more minute. Add the tomatoes and broth with their respective juices. Bring to a boil and simmer for 10 minutes. Combine green beans and coconut milk and simmer for another 5 minutes until tender. Combine lime juice and the rest of the green onions. Serve hot. Enjoy!

Farmers' Market Pizza

This pizza recipe is surely going to make your taste buds tingle with joy.

Ingredients

Tomato sauce

1 tablespoon of canola, plus some for oiling grill
3 plum tomatoes
2 tablespoons of oregano, fresh
1 tablespoon of red wine vinegar
1 tablespoon of olive oil
2 garlic cloves, minced
½ teaspoon of salt

½ teaspoon of red pepper flakes

Pizza

1½ cups of broccoli florets, large
1 red bell pepper, small and sliced
1 yellow bell pepper, small and sliced
½ red onion, cut into rings
¼ cup of canola oil
1 Par-Baked Pizza Crust
¼ teaspoon of black pepper, ground

Method

Oil the grill grate and preheat on medium heat. Make tomato sauce by brushing canola oil on the tomatoes. Grill them for 5 minutes. Make the puree of tomatoes, vinegar, garlic, salt, pepper, red chili flakes and oregano in a blender. Shift to bowl. Make pizza by tossing broccoli, onion, bell peppers, canola oil into a bowl. Shift them in grill basket and grill for 5-7 minutes. Slice the bell peppers. Spread tomato sauce on the crust and top with vegetables, grill and cook for 5 more minutes. Enjoy!

Herbed Macadamia-Almond Cheese

Make your own flavored cheese that you can add to variety of dishes, especially if you have a lactose intolerant member in your family.

Ingredients

Cheese base

1 cup macadamia nuts
1 cup almonds
½ teaspoon probiotic powder

Add-Ins

¼ cup red onion

¼ cup parsley
¼ cup pine nuts
2 tablespoons chives
2 tablespoons dill
2 tablespoons lemon juice
1 teaspoon sea salt
¼ teaspoon black pepper

Method

Soak the macadamia nuts and almonds in water for 8 hours. Drain and blend with fresh water and probiotic powder until creamy and smooth. Line small colander with wet cheese cloth to extract creamy nut mixture and set the colander to catch liquid in a dish. Fold excess of cloth on the mixture and set aside to ferment. Place 1 can over it after 2 hours to drain out excess liquid. Transfer the base into bowl and stir in the entire Add-Ins. Store in refrigerator till a week. Enjoy!

PROVENCAL TARTLETS

Tarts are delicious, healthy and a meal by themselves! Follow this easy recipe and get your hands on the deliciousness that they provide.

Ingredients

1½ cups green zucchini
1 cup yellow onion
2½ cups bell pepper
1 cup fennel bulb
4½ teaspoons olive oil
1½ teaspoons garlic
1 teaspoon thyme, oregano

1 cup roasted tomatoes
4 tablespoons Gaeta olives
1 tablespoon parsley
2 oz. Asiago cheese
3 tablespoons Parmesan cheese
Masa harina cream cheese dough

Method

Preheat oven to 400 degrees F. Toss the onion, zucchini, bell pepper and fennel with garlic, oil, oregano and thyme. Arrange vegetables on two baking sheets and roast in the preheated oven for 20 minutes. Transfer in bowl and set aside to cool. Add tomatoes, parsley, olives and cheese to the vegetables and toss. Reduce the oven temperature to 375 degrees. Scoop ¾ cup in each dough center. Fold edges inwardly and chill tarts for 10 minutes. Brush the tarts with some oil. Place on parchment paper. Bake for 30 minutes or until golden. Enjoy!

OKRA AND SWEET POTATO FRITTERS

A typical African cuisine styled fritters has an unusual combination of sweet potatoes and okra. It has a delicious flavor and goes well with stews and curries.

Ingredients

2½ cups of okra
1 cup sweet potato
¼ cup shallots
1 tablespoon honey

1 tablespoon soy sauce
½ cup yellow cornmeal
3 tablespoons canola oil

Method

Combine the sweet potato, okra, honey, shallot, soy sauce and corn meal in a bowl. Refrigerate for about 30 minutes. Wet your hands and divide mixture into 16 golf ball-size spheres and slightly flatten them. Heat the oil on medium heat in a large skillet. Cook fritters for 8 minutes while flipping once. Repeat with remaining oil and spheres. Serve warm fritters with dipping in soy sauce as desired. Enjoy!

Perfect Roasted Tomatoes

A delicious delicacy along with roasted juices delivers a fragmented appeal and emerges as a huge hit at snack parties. The dish can be stored in a fridge up to a week.

Ingredients

½ teaspoon salt
2 lbs. plum tomatoes, cored and cut into halves crosswise
1 tablespoon olive oil

¼ teaspoon ground pepper
4 sage leaves, chopped
5 thyme sprigs

Method

Preheat oven to 400 degrees F. Put tomatoes in a baking sheet lined with parchment paper, with its cut-side down. Brush with oil and sprinkle with sage, pepper, salt and thyme. Roast for 45 minutes until the skin blistered and flesh soft. Remove from oven and set aside to cool. Peel off skin and then serve. Enjoy!

Kefir "Orange Julius"

This drink is filling and satisfying to quench thirst as well as part-hungriness. This smooth lip smacking beverage will be a good start for a rocking party.

Ingredients

1 cup low-fat milk
1 teaspoon milk Kefir grains
1½ cups orange juice

1 teaspoon vanilla extract
¼ cup sugar
15 ice cubes

Method

Stir kefir grains in milk into pint sized glass jar. Cover jar with cheese-cloth in several layers and tie with rubber band. Store in room temperature until kefirs ferment and thicken. Keep an eye periodically on kefir's thickness. Once desired thickness achieved, strain kefir gently stirring, leaving only the kefir grains in strainer. Combine kefir with sugar, vanilla and orange juice in blender and pulse. Blend with ice cubes and then serve. Enjoy!

Almond-Cranberry Twist

These are great rolls to serve during dinner.

Ingredients

Filling
¾ cups toasted almonds
3 tablespoons unsalted butter
¼ cup sugar

⅛ teaspoon salt
2 teaspoons all-purpose flour
½ teaspoon almond extract
⅓ cup dried cranberries

Dough

2¼ cups all-purpose flour
3 teaspoons yeast

⅓ cup unsalted butter
⅓ cup sugar
1¼ teaspoon salt
2¼ cups whole-wheat flour

Method

Grind half almonds in food processor and add coarsely chopped other halves to it. Beat sugar, butter and salt in blender until smooth. Add flour and almond extract and beat again. Stir well in chopped almonds. Stir flour, yeast and warm water in bowl and prepare dough. Mix butter, salt and sugar into flour-yeast mixture and then add whole-wheat flour. Knead till smooth. Leave for 1 hour to rise. Set dough and make a rectangle on a parchment paper. Spread filling in the center and sprinkle cranberries. Roll as per desired shape and refrigerate. Brush some oil the over braids. Bake in oven until brown and cool. Enjoy!

SPARKLING LEMONADE

This soda preparation has to be started a week before it is planned to serve for best results.

Ingredients

1 cup sugar
A pinch of salt

2 cups fresh lemon juice
¼ teaspoon champagne yeast

Method

Boil 1 cup water in a small saucepan. Remove from heat and mix salt and sugar in it, till completely dissolved. Cool and add lemon juice and stir again. Pour the liquid using funnel into 2 liter soda bottle. Fill bottle with water leaving a 1 inch headspace. Add desired amount of sugar. Put yeast into mixture. Screw cap and shake well for even distribution of yeast. Keep bottle on room temperature for 5-7 days, checking lemonade periodically. Refrigerate the carbonated lemonade for 2 weeks. Open slowly and gradually to avoid bubbling-up. Store it in refrigerator for better results. Enjoy!

SAGE JULEP

A perfect drink to enjoy winter! A combination of sage mints with lemon taste tingles the taste-buds.

Ingredients

½ cup sage leaves, torn in halves, 6 whole for garnishing
5 lemons: 3 quartered, 2 for garnishing

6 tablespoons brown sugar
12 oz. unsweetened iced tea or bourbon
¾ cup seltzer water

Method

Freeze 6 empty tumblers. Take shaker and put 10 halved sage leaves, 1 tablespoons brown sugar and 2 lemon quarters for preparing each beverage individually. Mash together using the back of a spoon for 30 seconds, until aromatic. Add 4 ice cubes and top with bourbon or 2 oz. iced tea and 1oz. seltzer. Fill crushed ice in chilled tumblers and strain julep mixture over it from the shaker. At last garnish with sage leaf and lemon slice. Enjoy!

THE RED-HEADED MARY

A bright and vibrant surprising beverage for a perfect holiday brunch! It's a delicious beverage that can be customized according to your taste, make with carrot juice instead of tomato juice added with few dashes of hot sauce as per your choice or favorites. A leisure holiday gets more excited with an addition of such sumptuous drinks. The kids get equally amused to it very easily.

Ingredients

4 cups juice of fresh carrots
12 oz. vodka
¼ cup fresh lemon juice

2 tablespoons prepared or fresh horseradish
2 tablespoons vegetarian Worcestershire sauce

Method

Mix all ingredients and stir well until smooth and consistent in a pitcher. Add seasoning salt and a pinch of ground black pepper for desired taste. Store in a glass mason jar and refrigerate. Chill for around 1 hour and then serve. Enjoy!

GLUTEN-FREE PIZZA CRUST

Having a child, sibling, spouse or any other family member with a gluten allergy can be quite frustrating; both for them and for you. Let them enjoy the heaven known as "pizza" with this delicious gluten-free pizza crust

Ingredients

2½ teaspoons yeast
2 tablespoons flaxseed meal
1 teaspoon sugar
1 cup brown rice flour
1 cup white rice flour

1½ cups tapioca starch
2 teaspoons xanthan gum
1½ teaspoons salt
3 tablespoons olive oil

Method

Mix yeast, sugar and meal into warm water. Keep aside until it's cloudy. Whisk starch, gum, salt and rice flours in large bowl. Blend liquid into dry mixture to form dough. Add olive oil. Grease two pizza pans and place dough in them, while your hands are coated with oil. Press dough and shape to fit in pans. Keep aside for 1½ hours to rise. Preheat oven to 425 degrees F and par bake pizza pan for 15mins. Add desired toppings and bake again for more 7 minutes till cheese starts melting. Enjoy!

Black Bean and Chile Posole

An amazing Mexican stew which can be stored and enjoyed at whim!

Ingredients

2 (4-5 inches) dried Pasilla Chilies
2 medium, leeks, cut into 2 inches chunks
2 tablespoons olive oil
4 garlic cloves, minced
2 teaspoons ground cumin
1 teaspoon dried oregano
2 (15 oz.) cans of White Hominy, rinsed and drained
2 (15 oz.) cans of black beans, rinsed and drained

1 (15 oz.) can of tomatoes, fire-roasted

Garnishes (optional)

4 cups plain tortilla chips
2 small avocados, diced
2 tomatoes, diced
4 green onions, chopped
2 limes, sliced like wedges
½ cup cilantro, minced
Hot sauce

Method

Soften pasilla chilies. Once the seeds are discarded, puree it with the soaking liquid. Pass through a sieve and then pour the rest of the soaking liquid to it. Cut leek chunks into thin matchstick kind slices. Sauté the leeks until they are soft. To this, add the black beans, hominy, juicy tomatoes, and chili liquid with 6 cups of water. Cover the pan and boil. Once it starts to boil, simmer for 20 minutes. Arrange garnishes over the dish and serve hot. Enjoy!

Spicy Tofu Stew

Hot and sweet to the palette!

Ingredients

1 (16 oz.) jar red peppers, roasted
2 tablespoons chili-garlic sauce or sambal oelek chili paste (Huy Fong)
2 cups vegetable broth, low sodium

1(16 oz.) package tofu, cut into 1" cubes
2 medium bell peppers, thinly sliced
1 (10-oz) package baby spinach

Method

Mix chili paste and roasted peppers in food processor or blender until a smooth texture is achieved. Put in the soup pot with broth. Add 2 cups of water and boil. Add bell peppers, tofu cubes and simmer for 15 minutes or until the peppers feel tender. Mix spinach to it and reduce heat for five minutes. Make sure that the bright green color of spinach is maintained. Use salt and pepper for seasoning as per taste. Enjoy!

WHITE MOUNTAIN MIX

This gluten-free mix has a high calorific content and therefore, gives you an energy spike. High in its sodium content, the recipe is a sure shot winner. It takes no more than 30 minutes or less to assemble and gives you the amazing taste you would carry on your lips.

Ingredients

1 cup apple rings, dried, cut into bite-size pieces
1 cup pecan halves

¾ cup cranberries, dried
¾ cup pumpkin seeds
½ cup white chocolate chunks,

Method

There is no cooking time for the mix. For the preparation, it is essential that all the above written ingredients are mixed together. Put them all in a large bowl and mix well. Finally, make sure that the mix is stored in a re-sealable bag. Enjoy!

OVEN-FRIED TRUFFLE "CHIPS"

A rocking snack!

Ingredients

3 lbs. russet potatoes or Idaho, peeled
2 tablespoons olive oil
½ cup fresh parsley, chopped

¼ cup Parmesan cheese, grated (optional)
1 teaspoon truffle oil

Method

Cut the potatoes in to English style' chips-½ inch thick sticks. Immerse them in a large dish with salted water, covering them completely. Bring the water to a boil for 2 minutes and drain and cool. In an oven (pre-heated to 425 degree Fahrenheit) arrange parchment paper and baking paper. In a large bowl, toss the potatoes and oil. Spread this in a single layer on the baking sheet of the oven and shuffle in top and bottom racks each for 10 minutes. Season with salt, pepper and toss with parmesan, parsley and truffle oil. Enjoy!

MUSHROOM WONTON SOUP

Fabulous wantons with mushrooms!

Ingredients

1 12 oz. package of mushrooms, sliced
6 medium sized carrots, 1 minced, 5 sliced thinly

½ head bok choy, thinly sliced-2, rest minced
6 tablespoons fresh chives, chopped
1 tablespoon black bean sauce prepared

2 teaspoons sesame oil
4 cups mushroom broth, prepared

2 teaspoons soy sauce, low sodium
24 wanton wrappers (Twin Dragon Brand)

Method

Put aside 1 cup mushroom sliced and mince the remaining. Mix it with minced bok choy and add the chives, minced carrot, oil and black bean sauce to make 1and half cup mix. In the mushroom broth, add 2 cups of water, soy sauce; boil. Add sliced mushrooms, carrots and bok choy; reduce temperature and simmer. Put wantons (wrappers with the mix) and add to the broth. Enjoy!

CRISPY TOFU FINGERS

It is extremely lip smacking and yummy.

Ingredients

2 to16 oz. tofu, extra firm; drained
½ cup cornstarch
½ cup of Flaxseed meal (optional)
1 cup rice milk or soymilk(unsweetened)
2 cups panko breadcrumbs
½ cup flour

½ teaspoon paprika
½ teaspoon of dried sage
¼ teaspoon of garlic powder
¼ teaspoon of dried ginger
¼ teaspoon of onion powder
¼ teaspoon of black pepper(ground)

Method

Squeeze out extra moisture from tofu and cut in 16 fingers. Stir soymilk in flaxseed and cornstarch and put aside. Combine other ingredients and panko in another bowl. Immerse tofu fingers in the mixture of soymilk and later in panko mix. Ensure all sides are coated and bake in preheated oven for about 30 minutes. Make sure they are deep golden brown in color when served. Enjoy!

FRESH CORN AND TOMATILLO SALSA

Simple, yet lovely and smart cooking!

Ingredients

1½ cups Fresh Tomatillos, husked and cut
1½ cups Corn kernels fresh
6 tablespoons Cilantro, chopped

1 tablespoon Jalapeno chili, seeded
1 tablespoon Lime juice fresh

Method

Put tomatillos in a bowl and microwave on high power for 2 minutes. In order to cool very quickly, put in a freezer. Leave it there for 10 minutes. In a non-stick skillet heated over medium high heat, put corn, stir for a couple of minutes. Put in a larger plate and put in the freezer to cool quickly. This will take 10 minutes too. In a bowl, mix cilantro, lime juice and cilantro. Mix the corn and tomatillo sauce too, temper with seasonings like salt and pepper and serve. Enjoy!

MUSHROOM SLIDERS

Healthy and filling!

Ingredients

Sturdy homemade buns- as per requirement
½ cup Olive oil
3 tablespoons Red wine vinegar
1 tablespoon Dijon mustard
1 tablespoon Italian seasoning
1 teaspoon Worcestershire sauce
(vegetarian)

2 cloves of Garlic, chopped finely
24 large Baby bella mushrooms, stemmed
6 Deli slices of Gouda cheese, cut in
quarters
24 Tomatoes, sliced thinly
24 Lettuce leaves, torn slider-size

Method

Mix garlic, oil, mustard, Worcestershire sauce, Italian seasoning and vinegar in a bowl. Toss mushrooms in it to coat well. Marinate for 1 hour. In a pre-heated oven, bake mushrooms till the moisture is evaporated. To assemble, split a bun in half, arrange mushroom and Gouda cheese and toast. Put tomato and lettuce and cover with other half of bun and serve. Enjoy!

JACKFRUIT GYROS

Warmed pitas and hot jackfruit filling- perfect!

Ingredients

1 tablespoon Vegan margarine
1 large Onion, sliced thinly
1 20 oz. can Young jackfruit in brine,
rinsed, drained and in shreds
¾ cup Vegetable broth

4 tablespoons Lemon juice
2 teaspoons Dried oregano
1 teaspoon Soy sauce, low sodium
¾ teaspoon Coriander, ground

Method

Take a skillet and heat margarine till it starts to sizzle. Add onion and sauté till it softens (3-4 minutes). Add jackfruit and cook for 20 minutes. It should either get caramelized or get brown in color. Mix broth, oregano, half the lemon juice, coriander and soy sauce. Use seasoning like salt and pepper as per taste. Simmer till the liquid can no longer be seen or for 10-15 minutes. Put in the remaining lemon juice. Enjoy!

GRILLED VEGETABLE WRAP

Amazing tortilla- a vegetables filled delight!

Ingredients

12 thin Asparagus spears, trimmed
1 red Bell pepper, ½" strips size cut
1 Zucchini or summer squash, cut into rounds
1 clove of Garlic, chopped finely
½ teaspoon Red chili sauce (sriracha)

1 tablespoon Olive oil
½ cup White bean
2 (8-inch) Tortillas whole grain
6 Basil leaves
8 Red onion, thinly sliced
1 cup Baby arugula leaves

Method

In a pre-heated broiler or grill, mix together bell pepper, asparagus, oil and squash. Put seasonings as per taste. Mash together chili sauce, garlic and beans in a bowl till smooth. To assemble, put bean mixture in tortilla, top with basil leaves, roasted veggies, onion slices and arugula. Roll tightly, chill and serve. Enjoy!

SPICY BANH MI

A proper breakfast should always be heavy and filling. This veg-sandwich is tasty and involves intake of lot of fresh vegetables along with flavored tofu.

Ingredients

¼ cup of rice vinegar (can substitute with apple cider vinegar)
2 teaspoon of agave nectar, honey or sugar
½-1 teaspoon of flakes of red pepper
¼ cup of daikon radish, shredded
¼ cup of carrot, shredded
½-1 baguette (French or Vietnamese), lengthwise split into half
1 tablespoon of mayonnaise, low-fat

1 teaspoon of chili sauce (red)
1 teaspoon of tamari or soy sauce (low sodium)
½ cup of baked tofu (Asian flavored), thinly sliced, or fried into tofu cubes
2-6 inch strips of cucumber
6 cilantro sprigs
6 cherry tomatoes, sliced thinly
4 lettuce leaves

Method

Add vinegar, flakes of red pepper and honey in a bowl. Add carrot and radish to the mixture to prepare a topping. Mix well and leave for 15-30 minutes. Stir them continuously until it's combined. Now the oven should be preheated to about 350 degrees F. bake the baguette in oven till its crisp for 3-5 minutes. Let it cool down. Spread the mayonnaise on both sides of bread. Sprinkle the tamari and the red chili over it. Fill in the bread with cucumber, cilantro and tofu. Now the radish and carrot sauce should be drained onto the vegetables and spread it on them evenly. Garnish with lettuce and tomatoes and add salt and pepper to taste. Finally before serving press the baguette (top- half) on the sandwich. Enjoy!

KUNG PAO SLIDERS

It is a prize winning appetizer, easy to cook and a treat to your taste buds.

Ingredients

Sliders

1 14-oz. pkg. of tofu (extra-firm), patted dry
4 tablespoons of soy sauce, low sodium
2 tablespoons. of cane sugar (natural)
2 teaspoons of sesame oil, toasted
1 teaspoon of cornstarch
16 wheat buns

Slaw

3 tablespoons of soy sauce (low sodium)
2 tablespoons of vegan mayonnaise

2 tablespoons of peanut butter (creamy and natural)
5 teaspoons of cane sugar, natural
2 tablespoons of rice vinegar
2 teaspoons of sesame oil, toasted
1 teaspoon clove of minced garlic
⅛ teaspoon of black pepper, ground
1 pinch of cayenne pepper
4 8-oz of julienned carrots
2 8-oz of julienned zucchini
¼ cup of finely chopped peanuts (dry and roasted)

Method

At first, to prepare the sliders the tofu should be sliced lengthwise, then halve the slices to increase the number. Whisk together the soy sauce, oil, sugar and cornstarch in a small bowl. Pour on the tofu until completely covered and let it cool down for about 1 hour.

Now for the slaw whisk together the soy sauce, peanut butter, mayonnaise, vinegar, sugar, garlic, oil, cayenne and pepper, in a separate bowl. Slowly stir in the zucchini, carrots and peanuts. Leave it for cooling. The oven should be preheated to 375°F. The Baking sheet should be coated with the cooking spray. Drain in the tofu, and transfer to the already prepared coated baking sheet. Bake for 25 minutes. Flip the whole tofu and bake for 20-25 minutes more until crispy. Before serving, fill in the buns with sliced tofu and 2 tablespoons of slaw. Enjoy!

TASTY TOFU PATTIES

When pre grated carrots are used, this recipe can be prepared even faster.

Ingredients

¼ cup of vegan mayonnaise
¼ cup of onion, finely chopped
¼ cup of chopped parsley
2 teaspoon of dried tarragon
1 teaspoon of Dijon mustard
1 14-oz. pkg. of firm tofu
1 4-oz. can of rinsed and finely chopped mushrooms (sliced and drained)

⅓ cup of carrots, grated
4 finely chopped tomatoes (sun-dried in oil) drained
1 cup of breadcrumbs
1 16-oz. jar of tomato sauce, already prepared

Method

Whisk together the onion, parsley, mayonnaise, mustard and tarragon in a small bowl. Prepare a mixture by mashing tofu with fork. Stir in carrots, tomatoes and mushrooms. Fold in the breadcrumbs. Heat a large sized skillet after coating with cooking spray. Scoop in the tofu mixture onto the warm skillet in ¼th -cup of dollops. Cook for about 5 to 7 minutes until the patties are brownish golden. Flip the patties, and repeat the process. Cook as many patties required following the procedure and before serving top each patty with ¼ cup of tomato sauce. Serve in a plate. Enjoy!

Coconut Lentils

A dish generally enjoyed during the New Year, as according to myths the lentils gift wealth and fortune.

Ingredients

¼ cup of coconut flakes, unsweetened
1 tablespoon of coconut oil
1½ cups of chopped yellow onion
½ teaspoon of ground ginger
½ teaspoon of ground turmeric

¼ teaspoon of ground allspice
2 tablespoons. of tomato paste
1 cup of green lentils (French)
¼ cup of raisins
2 teaspoons of lime juice

Method

The oven should be preheated to 350°F. Arrange the coconut flakes on a baking sheet and toast them for around 4 to 6 minutes until golden. Set them aside. Heat the coconut oil in a large sized skillet. Add the chopped onions, and sauté to about 5-7 minutes till the onions are tender. Stir in turmeric, ginger and allspice for 30 seconds till its fragrance is prominent. Stir in and sauté tomato paste, again for another 30 seconds. Add 1 cup of water to the pan, and scrape out any brown colored bits if present. Add raisins, lentils and 2 cups of water. Boil them and leave for 30 minutes in a covered vessel. Now again cook for another 10-15 minutes unless the lentils soften. Add the lime juice and finally sprinkle pepper and salt to enhance the taste. Garnish each of the serving with 2 teaspoons of toasted coconut. Enjoy!

Portobello Cheeseburgers

These juicy burgers will simply take your heart away.

Ingredients

2 tablespoons of Bragg Aminos (Liquid)
2 tablespoons of red wine
4 oil-packed tomatoes, (sun-dried and drained)
1 tablespoon of oil reserved
1 teaspoon of Dijon mustard
⅛ teaspoon of ground black pepper (fresh)

8 Portobello mushrooms, large (stems and gills removed)
1 medium sized onion
4 oz. of goat cheese (garlic-herb)

Method

Whisk together the 1 tablespoon of oil with the tomatoes, wine, mustard, liquid aminos, pepper and ½ cup of water in a bowl. Pour over the mushrooms, and let it marinate for around 10 minutes. Heat up a grill pan. Initially grill the bottom side of the mushrooms for 4 minutes; then the onion rings for 5 minutes. On a platter, transfer the mushrooms with the bottom side pointing up where each mushroom should be filled in with 1 onion ring, 1 oz. of cheese and 1 tomato. Repeat the process for all other mushrooms left. Grill burgers for 10 minutes more, until cooked thoroughly. Enjoy!

YELLOW SPLIT PEA DAL

This is a classic Indian recipe which can be cooked easily in a pressure cooker and can be enriched by adding cauliflower and broccoli.

Ingredients

2 tablespoons of coconut oil
1 cup of finely chopped yellow onion
2 tablespoons of 6 cloves of minced garlic
½ cup of carrots, finely chopped
1 tsp. of cumin seeds

1 tsp. of turmeric powder
2 teaspoons of flakes of red pepper
1½ cups of yellow split peas (dried)
2 tablespoons of lemon juice
½ cup of cilantro leaves (optional)

Method

Preheat a rice cooker for 2-3 minutes. Pour in coconut oil and heat for 1 more minute. Add garlic onion, and carrots, and cook for 5-6 minutes till the vegetables become tender. Add flakes of red pepper, turmeric and cumin and cook for 1 minute more. Adjust the rice cooker settings so that the cooking process occurs slowly. Now, pour into the cooker the split peas and continuously keep on adding 4 cups of water by stirring. Add pepper and salt if desired. Finally, cover the pressure cooker and let it cook for 3-4 hours. If desired, the dal can be thinned by adding water. Before serving add lemon juice after garnishing with cilantro. Enjoy!

ARUGULA AND PEACH SALAD

The tangy taste of this salad makes it stand out from the rest of the salads usually made.

Ingredients

10 cups of arugula
4 sliced and pitted peaches
2 cups of finely chopped green bell peppers
⅔ cup of slivered almonds
2 tablespoons of olive oil
2 tablespoons of white balsamic vinegar
1 tablespoon of orange juice (fresh)

½ teaspoons of orange zest, grated
¼ teaspoons of salt
⅛ teaspoons of cayenne pepper

Method

Combine together the peaches, bell pepper, arugula and almonds in a large sized bowl. Separately, whisk together the olive oil, freshly prepared orange juice, the grated orange zest, the balsamic vinegar, cayenne pepper and salt, in another bowl. Before serving, the salad should be tossed properly along with the dressing. Enjoy!

CABBAGE CALZONES

This preparation requires pizza dough. This is a derivative of an Italian recipe.

Ingredients

¾ cup of 4 oz. of red potatoes (each made into ½-inch pieces)
2 cups of ¼ head of sliced and cored green cabbage
1 Tbs. of olive oil
1 cup of finely diced small onion
4 teaspoons of minced clove garlic
1½ tsp. of dried oregano

1 15-oz.can of chopped tomatoes
8 pitted and coarsely chopped Kalamata olives
2 teaspoons of red wine vinegar
3 Tbs. of fresh and chopped parsley
1 16-oz. package of pizza dough (already prepared)

Method

Boil a large sized pot of saline water. Add the potatoes, and cook until they soften. Now, add the cabbage to the pot and cook until tender. Drain the water and keep it aside. Warm oil in a skillet. Into the skillet now add onion, and cook for 5 minutes until softens. Next, add oregano and garlic, and cook for 1 minute. Add tomatoes, and keep on cooking till the mixture has mostly dried up. Add vinegar and olives, and cook for 3 more minutes. Now, gently add the parsley, cabbage and potatoes into the mixture, keep stirring. Add pepper and salt to enhance the taste. Keep it for cooling. The oven should be preheated to 425°F. Use the cooking spray to coat the baking sheet. Cut the dough into 8 pieces, and roll each piece into an 8-inch of diameter circle. Now place the ½ cup of filling on the below half of each diameter of the circle, leaving around ¾-inch of border surrounding the edges. Fold the dough containing the filling, and pinch the ends together so that it gets sealed. Repeat the process with the remaining pieces. Make 3 tiny slits at the top of each calzone. The calzones just prepared should be transferred to the greased baking sheet. Bake until the calzones turn golden brown. Serve. Enjoy!

HAWAIIAN PIZZA

This is a gluten free recipe and can be refrigerated for a long time. Pizza is a fast food which can be easily prepared at home. The pizza sauce and the molten cheese make one to crave for it more.

Ingredients

1¼ cups of pizza sauce
1 par-baked pizza crust (Gluten-free)

1½ cups of shredded mozzarella
½ cup of fresh pineapple, diced

1 gluten-free veggie-burger patty (crumbled and cooked)

2 teaspoons of flakes of red pepper

Method

The oven should be preheated to 425°F. Spread the pizza sauce on the par-baked crust. Top with diced pineapple, shredded mozzarella, veggie-burger patty (crumbled), and flakes of red pepper. Bake for 5-7 minutes till the cheese melts and the toppings turn golden brown. Before serving, garnish with arugula. Enjoy!

GRILLED SALAD PIZZA

A grilled salad is something which is a recipe which tasty yet healthy.

Ingredients

2 tablespoons of balsamic vinegar
2 teaspoons of honey
1 teaspoon of Dijon mustard
½ teaspoons of small clove of minced garlic
3 tablespoons of olive oil
1 Chewy Pizza Dough

3 tablespoons of Parmesan cheese, grated
1 cup of arugula
1 cup of romaine lettuce, sliced
1 cup of head of red endive, sliced and halved
½ cup of fresh fennel, thinly sliced
¼ cup of red onion, thinly sliced

Method

At first to prepare the vinaigrette: Whisk together the honey, garlic, vinegar and mustard. Coat with oil, and add pepper and salt to taste. Set it aside for 30 minutes. Next for the pizza, prepare the chewy pizza dough, and drizzle grated Parmesan. The oven should be preheated to 350°F. Then bake the pizza for about 25 minutes till the bottom is brown and crispy. Brush with 3 tabespoons of Vinaigrette at the bottom of the pizza. Now, with the rest of the vinaigrette, toss lettuce, fennel, arugula, onions and endive. Use the arugula mixture as the topping for the pizza. Finally, till the vegetables starts wilting, broil them for around 2-3 minutes. Garnish with the Parmesan curls and serve immediately. Enjoy!

EDAMAME PÂTÉ SANDWICHES

There is nothing like a cozy afternoon with this sandwich and drinks. The pate is a multipurpose sauce and can be used as a spread over bread or on crackers or even can be used as a dip.

Ingredients

1¼ cups of shelled edamame, frozen and thawed
½ cup of walnuts
⅓ cup of packed mint leaves
1 chopped green onion
½ teaspoon of salt

3 tablespoon of lemon juice
8 slices of bread (whole-grain)
2 cups of arugula
4 jarred red peppers, roasted and drained
2 small thinly sliced cucumbers

Method

Process the walnuts, green onions, thick edamame and the mint leaves after adding into it a pinch of salt to enhance the taste. The process should be continued until the ingredients are finely chopped. Now add the lemon juice and 3 tablespoons of water to the processor while it is running. Now, smoothen them thoroughly. Spread ⅓ cup of pâté over both the sides of each of the 4 bread slices. Finally, add ½ cup of arugula, cucumbers and 1 roasted pepper to each. Combine all the 8 slices and the sandwich will be ready to serve. Enjoy!

OVEN FRIED TRUFFLE CHIPS

These are short and thick and are actually fries baked in the oven that show resemblance with the British chips.

Ingredients

3 lbs. of peeled russet potatoes or Idaho
2 tablespoons of olive oil
½ cup of fresh parsley, chopped

¼ cup of Parmesan cheese, grated
1 teaspoon of truffle oil

How to chook?

Slice the potatoes into British style chips. You will get them if you cut the chips into sticks having thickness of 0.5 inches. Transfer the chips to a large saucepan which is already filled with salted water. After boiling the water for around 2 minutes, drain it and cool the pan. Set the temperature to 425 degree Fahrenheit for preheating the oven. After that, use the parchment paper for lining 2 baking sheets. Take oil in a big bowl and toss potatoes in it. Spread them in a line on the baking sheets and then bake them for half an hour. You have to stir the potatoes and change the baking sheets from one rack to another frequently. Then put the potatoes in a bowl for tossing them with truffle oil, parmesan and parsley. Enjoy!

BROCCOLI RAAB WITH SPICY PEANUT-MISO DRESSING

This typical Asian–styling garnishing reflects West-meets-East makeover to broccoli raab. The salad can be served as a light meal or an additional delicacy.

Ingredients

1 lb. Broccoli rab with trimmed ends
3 tablespoons Natural peanut butter (chunky style)
1 tablespoon Rice vinegar

2 teaspoons Miso (sweet white)
2 teaspoons Honey
½ teaspoon Chile-garlic sauce

Method

Boil about 2 inches of water in a large pan. Add broccoli and cover the pan. Cook for about 4 minutes. Flip once using tongs and cook for 4 more minutes, till the raab is tender and vibrant green. Drain water and let it cool. Cut stem into halves. Whisk 2 tablespoons water, peanut butter, honey, miso, chili-garlic sauce and vinegar together in a bowl. Pour gently over broccoli raab and toss for even distribution. Enjoy!

Miso-Roasted Eggplant Soup

This hearty blended soup has a creamy, rich base.

Ingredients

¼ cupMiso (sweet white)
¼ cup Orange juice
1 tablespoon Mirin
2 teaspoons Brown sugar
1 tablespoon Almond oil

2 medium Eggplants sliced into ¼inch size
1½ cups Onion
½ cup Almond milk
2 tablespoons Toasted almonds

Method

Use cooking spray to spray on foils lining 2 baking sheets. Preheat oven at 400 degrees F. Stir miso, brown sugar, orange juice, almond oil and mirin together in a bowl. Brush both surface of eggplants with the mixture. Arrange on baking sheet and top with slices of onions. Roast for 20 minutes till caramelized slightly. Transfer the whole preparation in a blender and combine with 2½ cups water and almond milk and pulse to smooth puree. Add more water for desired thickness. Sprinkle toasted sliced almonds. Enjoy!

Three-Herb Cherry Tomato Pizza

The ingredients are enough to make 1 large pizza rectangular in size or 2 small 11" round pizzas. The par baked pizza crusts can be kept up to 2 to 3 days in a fridge or for months in freezer.

Ingredients

1¼ cups Marinara sauce
1 Gluten-Free Pizza Crust par baked
8 oz. Mozzarella, fresh
1½ cups Cherry tomatoes, halved and sliced

¼ cup Parsley, fresh and chopped
¼ cup Basil, fresh and chopped
¼ cup Chives, chopped

Method

Preheat oven at 425 degrees F. Spread marinara sauce gently over pizza crust. Use fresh mozzarella and tomatoes as toppings. Bake for around 7 minutes till cheese begins bubbling. Remove from oven and place fresh basil, fresh parsley and chives as further toppings. Serve hot. Enjoy!

Spicy Cashew Cheese

This recipe will enable you to make 1 to 2 cups of a cream spread that can energize you for days. What is more fascinating that its flavor intensifies with time.

Ingredients

1 cup of raw cashews

3 tablespoons of lime juice

2 tablespoons of dehydrated onion, minced

2 teaspoons of lime zest, grated

¾ teaspoons of kosher salt

½ teaspoons of chipotle powder

½ teaspoons of ground coriander

½ teaspoons of ground cumin

½ teaspoons of garlic powder

Method

Keep the cashews in a big bowl and cover it with four cups of boiling water. Use a clean towel for covering it and then soak it for the next six hours. Drain the water and rinse the cashews. Mix the cashews with the other ingredients along with 1 tablespoons of cold water using a food processor or blender for around 5 minutes. Chill the smooth paste for 3 hours and you are ready to serve. Enjoy!

GRILLED SERRANO SALSA VERDE

The best thing about Grilled Serrano Salsa Verde is that it can be prepared in just half an hour or even lesser amount of time. Thus, if you are in a hurry and need something to add taste to other food items, this is perfect for you. It can be easily used as a topping for items like tacos, tofu, rice bowls and others.

Ingredients

1 bunch of fresh cilantro

¾ cups of olive oil

1 roasted or grilled serrano chili

1 tablespoon of champagne vinegar

1 large or 2 small garlic cloves in grilled form

Method

Use a bowl present in a food processor for mixing all the ingredients along with ¼ cup water. Just mix it until it becomes a smooth paste. Enjoy!

CASHEW CREAM

This is one of the easily toppings and can be used for bringing taste to different dishes. It is one of the best alternatives for sour cream, cream and cheese used in vegan and raw recipes. The below recipe will enable you to make 3 cups of cashew cream at a time, all of which can be preserved in the fridge for around 7 days.

Ingredients

2 cups of raw cashews

8 cups of boiling water

Method

Use eight cups of boiling water for covering 2 cups of raw cashews in a big bowl. After covering the bowl with a clean towel, let it stand for around 6-8 hours. Then drain the cashews and mix it with around half cup of cold water in a blender for 5 minutes. You can continue it till the cream becomes thick and smooth. Enjoy!

Berry-Apricot Salsa

Salsas are generally savory, but the above one is a sweet concoction and can be used as topping on pancakes and yoghurt. You can even use it as a sauce for ice creams.

Ingredients

1 cup of divided raspberries
2 tablespoons of apricot preserves
1 cup of fresh apricots, peaches or nectarines, in diced form

1 cup of blackberries
3 tablespoons of candied ginger, chopped

Method

Squash four raspberries in a medium sized bowl and stir in the apricot preserves for making sauce base. Mix the remaining raspberries, ginger, blackberries and fresh apricots. Keeping the berries intact, toss it carefully. You can even season it with pepper and salt if you want to. The flavors should be allowed to meld by letting the salsa stand for around 7-10 minutes. Enjoy!

Tuscan Pizza

Ingredients

1 cup of vegan pesto (already prepared)
1 Pizza crust, par-baked and gluten free
¾ cup of caramelized onions

½ cup of dried figs, thinly sliced
3 Tbs. of pine nuts
1 Tbs. of olive oil

Method

At first, the oven should be preheated to 425°F. The vegan pesto should be spread over the gluten-free and par baked pizza crust. The caramelized onions, thinly sliced dry figs, olive oil and the pine nuts should be used as a topping over the crust. When the dressing of the pizza will be ready, it should be baked for 5-7 minutes until the topping is soft, tender and warm enough. Now removing from the oven, serve the delicious Tuscan pizza hot and juicy. Enjoy!

Pico De Gallo Pizza

Ingredients

2 cups of tomato salsa (fresh)
1 pizza crust, par baked and gluten free
1¼ cups of queso blanco
1 cup of fire-roasted corn, frozen and thawed
1 sliced avocado

1 cup of lettuce (chopped watercress)

Method

At first the oven should be preheated to 425°F. The gluten free and par-baked pizza crust should be spread with tomato salsa. The roasted corn and the queso blanco should be used as a topping over the crust. Finally, the pizza should be baked for 5-7 minutes until the cheese melts and turns golden brown and the toppings are soft and tender. Removing from the oven, garnish it with the lettuce (or watercress) and the sliced avocado and serve the cheesy hot pizza. Enjoy!

THREE-PEA SALAD WITH MEYER LEMON VINAIGRETTE

For vinaigrette, if the oil to acid ratio is 2:1 rather than the usual 3:1, then it is perfect. The Meyer lemon makes this salad special.

Ingredients

Vinaigrette
3 tablespoons of lemon juice (Meyer lemons)
2 teaspoons of lemon zest (minced Meyer lemons)
½ teaspoons of salt
6 tablespoons of olive oil (extra virgin)

Salad
2 cups of garden peas (shelled, fresh or frozen)
2 cups of peas (sugar snap), cut into lengths of ¾-inches
1½ cups of 12 thinly sliced radishes
1 cup of 3 small sized and thinly sliced carrots
2 cups of pea shoot (baby arugula)

Method

At first for the Vinaigrette, whisk together the meyer lemon zest, salt and the meyer lemon juice. Slowly stir in the oil and continue the whisking unless the whole mixture is emulsified. This makes the vinaigrette which will be later used as the dressing.

Now to prepare the salad, take a large bowl of ice cold water. Separately boil a pot of salinated water. Into it, add the garden peas and the sugar snap peas. Boil the peas for around 1 minute. Then drain out the saline water and bath the peas with the ice cold water. Drain out that water as well. Now keep the boiled and bathed peas separately in a large sized bowl. Into that bowl, place the sliced carrots and radishes into the peas mixture. Before serving toss the whole mixture with about ¼ cup of vinaigrette or more according to the preference. Finally garnish with the pea shoots and serve. Enjoy!

SMOKED PORTOBELLO CLUB SANDWICH

This club sandwich makes a perfect lunch. It is easy to make at home but the vegetables used in this sandwich should be very thinly sliced so that it becomes easy for the person to handle it while eating.

Ingredients

1½ tablespoons of hickory wood chips (apple wood chips)

2 tablespoons of olive oil
1 tablespoon of lemon juice

2 large sized (6-inch) de-stemmed and de-gilled mushroom (Portobello) caps
6 thin slices of whole-wheat bread (white bread)

1 thinly sliced plum tomato
1 cup of romaine heart leaves, finely shredded
¼ cup of goat cheese, crumbled

Method

At first, the wood chips should be stove-top smoked. Then the lemon juice and the olive oil should be whisked together in a small sized bowl. Add pepper and salt to enhance the taste. Both the sides of the mushrooms should be bathed in the oil mixture just prepared. Now, the mushrooms are stove-topped and smoked for around 25 minutes till they are soft and tender and get a brownish tinge. Keep the mushrooms aside to cool down. The mushrooms should be now diagonally cut into pieces and arranged over the toasted slices of bread. Now the sliced tomato should also be added. Separately, the goat cheese, the rest of the oil mixture and the lettuce should be tossed and this topping should be used on the bread slices, along with the mushrooms and the tomatoes. Now close the sandwich with another toasted bread slice. Continue the process for the number of desired sandwiches to be prepared and finally before serving cut them into quarters. Enjoy!

SWISS MISS PIZZA

Ingredients

1 cup of squash (butternut) soup, already prepared
1 pizza crust, par-baked and gluten free
1½ cups of Swiss cheese, grated

1 cup of fennel, thinly sliced
1 cup of radicchio, thinly sliced
¼ cup of black olives, sliced

Method

The oven should be preheated to 425°F. The gluten-free and par-baked crust should be spread with the already prepared squash soup. The thinly sliced fennel, the sliced radicchio pieces and the sliced olives should be now used as a topping over the crust. The pizza with its dressing should be baked for 5-7 minutes, unless the cheese melts completely before the time is up. Finally the hot and juicy pizza is ready to be served. Enjoy!

SPINACH AND GOAT CHEESE BAKED VEGETARIAN OMELETS SANDWICHES

This recipe reminds us of the spring season. All the fresh vegetables add it all to the flavor. And the best part? No eggs!

Ingredients

2 teaspoons of olive oil
1 medium sized and thinly sliced leek

3 oz of 3 packed cups of spinach leaves (baby)

2 cups gram flour
2 large tomatoes. chopped
2 tablespoons of milk (low-fat)
½ cup of frozen peas

4 tablespoons of goat cheese (2 oz.), crumbled
2 tablespoons of parsley, chopped
4 slices of multigrain bread

Method

The oven should be preheated to 350°F. Warm oil in a small sized skillet onto which the leek should be added and cooked till it's soft. Slowly add ¾ cup of spinach leaves by stirring till they are wilted. Keep it aside. Now the gram flour and the milk should be whisked together in another bowl where goat cheese, tomatoes, parsley and the peas should be stirred in. Add pepper and salt onto it to enhance the taste. Now this gram flour mixture should be added to the spinach cooked in the skillet. Now all of these ingredients in the skillet should be transferred to the oven which should be baked for 15 minutes until the omelet is prepared. Now leaving it to cool to room temperature they should be cut into quarters like sandwich strips. Now the omelet strips should be arranged on the top of the bread slices. The remaining spinach can be used as a topping. Cut the bread slices into half and wrap up with plastic wraps. Refrigerate for a night. Serve the next day. Enjoy!

ZUCCHINI-GOAT CHEESE PIZZA

This pizza is lighter and cuts out on the calorie count immensely.

Ingredients

Pizza

2 tablespoons of olive oil
8 oz. (½ pkg.) of pizza dough (prepared and refrigerated)
1 3.5-oz. log of roughly chopped and thinly sliced goat cheese
1 peeled and thinly stripped zucchini
1 small sized bell pepper (red)

Sauce

1 6-oz. can of tomato paste
2 tablespoons of onion, finely minced
2 teaspoons of 2 cloves of minced garlic
2 teaspoons of dried oregano
2 teaspoons of olive oil
½ teaspoons of red wine (red wine vinegar)

Method

At first for the pizza the oven should be preheated to 450°F. Now, the pizza pan or the baking sheet should be bathed in with 1 tablespoon of oil. Spread the pizza dough in the already prepared pan. Secondly, to make the sauce all the ingredients should be stirred together in a small sized bowl. This sauce should be spread on the dough. Half of the goat cheese should be used as a topping. Now, spread the strips of zucchini on the goat cheese which should be topped with the rings of red bell pepper and again the rest of the goat cheese. Drip in the leftover olive oil. Now bake the crust for about 10-15 minutes till the cheese melts and gets a golden brown tinge. Leave for cooling and cut into pizza slices. Serve hot and juicy. Enjoy!

Peanut-Stuffed Okra Fingers

This is an Indian recipe ideal for those who savor bold flavors.

Ingredients

1 lb. or 24 okra pods, fresh
1 cup of peanuts (roasted and unsalted)
¼ cup of ½ small sized onion
2 cloves of garlic
1 1-inch piece of fresh ginger

1 deseeded jalapeno chili
½ tsp. of cumin
½ teaspoons of coriander
½ teaspoons of salt

Method

At first the oven should be preheated to 425°F. The baking sheet should be coated with the cooking spray or parchment paper should be used to line it. After chopping off the heads of okra, split them into half, lengthwise, using a paring knife. Now, the pods should be opened carefully, taking care not to tear them. Process the onions, ginger, garlic, peanuts, jalapenos, coriander, cumin and salt until they are coarsely chopped. Spoon the peanut mixture into the okra pods. Place them on the baking sheet and bake for around 15 minutes till the pods have tendered and get a brownish tinge. Serve warm. Enjoy!

Garlic Knot Pizza

Ingredients

⅓ cup of olive oil
½ cup of parsley leaves
4 cloves of garlic

1 pizza crust, gluten free and par-baked
½ cup of Parmesan cheese, grated

Method

At first the oven should be preheated to 425°F. The olive oil, garlic cloves and the parsley leaves should be blended and the oil bathed mixture is to be brushed over the gluten free and par-baked pizza crust. Make the dressing with grated Parmesan cheese, which should be used as a topping and then add pepper and salt to enhance the taste. Bake the pizza crust for 5-7 minutes until the topping is warm and cheesy. Serve the juicy pizza with molten cheese dripping from it. Enjoy!

Barbecue Bella Pizza

Ingredients

1¼ cups of barbecue sauce (thick and gluten-free)
1 pizza crust, gluten-free and par-baked
1½ cups of Cheddar cheese, shredded

¾ cup of bella mushrooms (baby), sliced
2 tablespoons of olive oil

Method

At first, the oven should be preheated to 425°F. The thick and gluten free barbeque sauce should be spread over the par-baked and the gluten free pizza crust. The shredded cheddar cheese and the sliced baby bella mushrooms should be used as the topping. The whole dressing should be bathed in with olive oil. Bake the crust for 5-7 minutes till the cheese is molten and gets a golden brown tinge. Serve hot and juicy. Enjoy!

SPRING SALAD DRESSED WITH AVOCADO AÏOLI

An aïoli sauce is creamy and achieves its texture from the avocado. This sauce can be a multipurpose sauce and can spread on breads, used as a dip or even as toppings.

Ingredients

12 potatoes (fingerling)
12 oz. of end trimmed asparagus
1 small sized avocado
⅓ cup of chives, chopped
3 tablespoons of lemon juice

2 tablespoons. of tarragon leaves (fresh)
1 teaspoons of honey
1 teaspoons of 1 minced clove of garlic
¼ cup of olive oil
½ cup of thinly sliced 6 radishes

Method

Boil a good amount of water and the fingerling potatoes in a covered saucepan. Heat it on a stove till the potatoes are soft. Remove the potatoes from the saucepan and bath them with ice cold water. Drain out the water. Now add the trimmed asparagus to the boiling water and cook for 1-2 minutes. Again, when they are soft and green enough take them out and bath in with ice water and let the water drain out. Now, form a blended mixture with the lemon juice, ¼ cup of chives, avocado, honey, tarragon leaves and garlic by processing them and till they are emulsified properly. Add pepper and salt to enhance the taste. Now arrange large salad plates and spread 2 tablespoons of avocado sauce thickly on the streaks using the back side of a spoon. Cut the potatoes lengthwise and arrange them and the asparagus on the plates. Finally use the rest of the chives and the radish slices as garnish and serve. Enjoy!

ROASTED CHICKPEAS WITH CAJUN SPICES

This is a dish which can melt your heart. The chickpeas maybe a bit sweeter but more pepper can be added to add on to the spice.

Ingredients

2 teaspoons paprika
⅛ teaspoon of garlic powder
1 pinch of cayenne pepper

2-15 oz. cans of 3 cups of cooked
chickpeas, (low-sodium)
1 tablespoon of olive oil

Method

At first, the oven should be preheated to 400°F. Slowly the garlic powder, paprika and the pinch of cayenne should be stirred in a small sized bowl. Keep the mixture aside. The rinsed chickpeas should be pat dried and spread on a baking sheet. Then, baked for around 40 minutes and placed on another bowl and bathed in with oil as a coating. Now, dress the chickpeas with the spice mixture and gently stir in to create a nice coating. Pepper and salt maybe added to enhance the taste. The temperature of the oven should be decreased to 300°F and again the chickpeas should be baked till they are crisp and gain a golden tinge. Keep it for cooling and finally serve. Enjoy!

*R*USSIAN BLACK BREAD

This black bread is a perfect sandwich slice for breakfast or for a quick snack.

Ingredients

2¼ teaspoon Yeast
¾ teaspoon Sugar
2 cups Rye-flour (Bob's Red Mill)
2 cups All-purpose flour
1¼ tablespoons Caraway-seeds
1 teaspoon Coffee-beans,
1 teaspoon onion powder
1 teaspoon salt

¼ teaspoon Fennel-seeds
2 tablespoons Fleischmann's white vinegar
2 tablespoons Molasses
2 tablespoons Margarine
½ oz. Chocolate
Oil
½ teaspoon Cornstarch

Method

Take a bowl and stir warm water, sugar, and yeast. Whisk caraway seeds, ½-cup flour, coffee, rye-flour, salt, fennel-seeds, and onion-powder in another bowl. Combine vinegar, chocolate, water, molasses and margarine in saucepan and low-heat until melted. Add melted-mixture into rye flour-mixture. Combine with yeast-mixture and stir. Add remaining flour until a smooth dough forms. Let it rise until doubles in size. Preheat oven and grease-oil onto a baking-sheet. Bake ball-shaped dough for 50 minutes. Boil ¼-cup water with cornstarch and cook. Brush mixture over loaf-top. Bake for 2-3 minutes. Enjoy!

*T*OFUSH AND TARTAR SAUCE

The delicious tasting dish is a hit at parties!

Ingredients

Tartar Sauce

1 cup Soymilk 1cup
1 tablespoon Wine-vinegar
½ tablespoon Dijon-mustard
2 cups Oil
¼ cup Shallots
¼ cup Capers
1-2 nos. Cornichon-pickles
2 tablespoons Dill

Tofush

14 oz. Tofu (2nos)
1 cup White-wine
¼ cup Lemon-juice
1½ teaspoon Salt
3 Nori-sheets, halved
1 cup Plain-flour
⅓ cup Corn-flour
¼ teaspoon Black-pepper
1 cup Vegan-ale
6 cups Oil
Lemon-wedges

Method

For Tartar Sauce: Blend mustard, soymilk, and vinegar well. Add oil. Combine with capers, shallot, dill, and pickles. Refrigerate.

For Tofush: Divide tofu into 3 parts. Stir lemon juice, salt and wine in baking dish. Add tofu. While flipping once, marinate for an hour. Drain on paper towels and dry. Wrap each slab with nori and attach with toothpick. Whisk corn flour, flour, salt, and pepper in bowl. Whisk again in ale until just smooth. Heat oil in oven. Lower batter coated nori-tofu and turn twice to fry until golden-brown. Remove in paper-towels and discard toothpick. Serve with lemon and sauce. Enjoy!

GLUTEN-FREE SAGE CORNBREAD

Ingredients

1 cup Yellow cornmeal
¾ cup Brown rice flour
¼ cup Potato starch
2½ teaspoons Baking powder
½ teaspoon Baking soda

½ teaspoons Salt
1-2 tablespoons Fresh sage (chopped)
1 cup Low-fat buttermilk
¼ cup Honey
1 tablespoon Melted butter

Method

Preheat the oven to 400 degrees F. Grease baking dish using cooking spray. Whisk rice flour, salt, baking powder, cornmeal, baking soda, and starch together in bowl. Add sage and stir. Whisk honey and butter milk and combine dry-mixture to wet-mixture. Let rest for 5 minutes. Spread butter in prepared dish and bake for half an hour until brown and crisp. Brush with melted butter and slice after cooling. Enjoy!

CREAMY SWISS CHARD GRATINS

Large gratin can also be prepared instead of small cup-size.

Ingredients

½ cup Breadcrumbs
⅓ cup Parmesan-cheese
2 teaspoons Olive-oil
2 tablespoons Butter
1 lb. Swiss-chard, sliced

1 cup Leeks, sliced
2 cloves of Garlic
1 tablespoon Plain-flour
1 cup Low-fat milk
½ teaspoon Worcestershire sauce

Method

Preheat oven. Coat custard-cups using cooking-spray. Combine 1 tbsp cheese, 1 tsp oil, and breadcrumbs in bowl. Heat 1 tsp oil and 1 tbs butter on medium-heat in a skillet. Add leeks and chard-stems. Cook until softened. Uncover and sauté. Cook chard-leaves until full-wilted. Stir garlic and transfer in a bowl. Heat leftover butter in a saucepan. Whisk flour and milk and cook until sauce thickens. Remove pan and add Worcestershire sauce with remaining cheese. Combine chard-mixture and split them into custard-cups. Add breadcrumbs toppings. Bake for 19 minutes until gratin bubbly and browned. Enjoy!

OVERNIGHT INJERA

This overnight Injera goes well with sandwich wraps or vegetable stews.

Ingredients

2 cups Teff flour
½ cup Gluten-free flour mix
2 teaspoons Dry yeast
A pinch of Fenugreek

A pinch of Cumin
½ teaspoon Salt
1 tablespoon Honey

Method

Whisk yeast, flour-mix, Teff-flour, cumin and fenugreek together in bowl. Stir well with ½ cups warm water. Use kitchen-towel to cover it for a day until it smells yeasty and top bubbling. Stir honey and salt in it. Add water as required to resemble like thin pan-cake batter. Heat a large skillet on medium-heat. Pour 3-quarter batter spread in a way thinner than pan-cake and thicker than a crepe. Cook for a minute until Injera filled with bubbles. Separate edges using spatula and place in a plate. Cover and repeat with the leftover batter. Enjoy!

PUMPKIN-PEAR BREAD

Ingredients

1¼ cup Sugar
1 cup Flour(all purpose)
1 cup Pastry(whole-wheat)
2 teaspoons Baking powder
2 teaspoons Ground cinnamon
1 teaspoon Ground nutmeg
1 teaspoon Baking soda
¼ teaspoon Salt

½ cup Vegetable oil
½ cup Low-fat milk
Pumpkin puree (oven roasted)- ¾ cup/ pumpkin puree (unsweetened)- ½ (15 oz. can)
1 teaspoon Vanilla extract
1 can of Pears(15 oz. drained and diced)

Method

Make sure that the oven is pre heated to 350 degrees Fahrenheit and a pan of a 9 inch sprayed with cooking spray. In a bowl, whisk sugars, baking powder, flours, cinnamon, baking soda, nutmeg and salt. Put aside.. Mix oil and milk, then vanilla and pumpkin. Put in the flour mixture into milk-oil mix and stir-in pears. Put the batter in the loaf pan and bake for 45-55 minutes. Enjoy!

CRISPY TOFU FINGERS

Delicious tofu fingers which are baked and hence are low in calories. You can even store them for future consumption!

Ingredients

2 (16 oz.) Tofu
½ cup Cornstarch
½ cup Flaxseed meal
1 cup Soymilk or rice milk
2 cups Panko breadcrumbs
¼ cup Flour(all purpose)

½ teaspoon Paprika
½ teaspoon Dried sage
¼ teaspoon Garlic powder/granulated garlic
¼ teaspoon Dried ginger
¼ teaspoon Onion powder
¼ teaspoon Black pepper(ground)

Method

Squeeze out extra moisture from tofu by placing it between two heavy cutting boards. Cut 16 even fingers out of it. Oven should be pre-heated to 350 degrees. Put flaxseed meal and cornstarch in a bowl and combine soymilk. Put aside. Mix panko and all the other ingredients in another bowl. To assemble in the baking dish, pick up the tofu fingers; dip in the soymilk mix and then the panko mix. Put them straight into the baking sheets pre-sprayed with cooking spray. Bake them for 20-25 minutes or until golden brown. Enjoy!

SOURDOUGH SANDWICH

Ingredients

3 cups Bread Flour (divided)
1¼ cup Yeast (quick rising) like Fleischmann's RapidRise

1¼ cup Shortcut Sourdough Starter
2 tablespoons Brown Sugar (light)
1½ teaspoons Salt

Method

Mix 1½ cups of bread flour and yeast. In a separate bowl, mix brown sugar, starter and ¾ cup lukewarm water. To this add the yeast-flour mixture, loosely cover and let it sit overnight. The following day, stir salt and another cup of flour in the sponge. Keep adding some flour and roll out to a cylinder shape. In a loaf pan with some cooking spray sprayed, put the dough inside and let it rise for an hour. Preheat oven to 375 degrees Fahrenheit. With a serrated knife, cut ½ inch deep slashes lengthwise into the dough. Bake for 45 minute and cool for another 45 minutes. Slice and serve. Enjoy!

CRANBERRY-PECAN PIE

This is a traditional pecan-pie with a twist of fresh cranberries!

Ingredients

1½ cup Pecan Halves
1 cup Thawed cranberries
1 9 inch Prepared pie-crust
⅓ cup Sugar
⅓ cup Brown sugar(dark)
⅓ cup Honey

1 tablespoon Margarine or butter
2 teaspoons Orange zest(grated)
½ teaspoon Vanilla extract
½ teaspoon Ground cinnamon
¼ teaspoon Salt

Method

The oven should be preheated to 350 degrees Fahrenheit. On a baking sheet, the pecans are to be toasted for no more then 5-7 minutes. Make sure they are just light brown and fragrant. Also, crush lightly the cranberries to be spread lowest in the pie-crust. In a bowl, whisk sugar honey, brown sugar, and vanilla, orange zest, cinnamon, vanilla and salt. Add pecans, and then pour in the entire thing over the cranberries. Make sure that the pecans and cranberries are evenly distributed. The time for baking is 40-45 minutes. Serve while warm. Enjoy!

Guava Cheese Tamales

Bring home the Caribbean flavor and make the brunches super successful!

Ingredients

Tamales

1(8-oz packet) Corn Husks
4 oz. Cream Cheese (reduced fat and softened)
2 oz.Cotija Cheese(grated)
1 cup Guava paste
2 teaspoons Lime juice(fresh)

Masa

3½ cups Masa harina

1½ teaspoons Baking powder
1 teaspoon Salt
¼ teaspoon Ground cinnamon
⅛ teaspoon Ground nutmeg (fresh)
5 tablespoons Butter (unsalted and softened)
5 tablespoons Vegetable shortening
½ cup Brown sugar (light)
1 cup Apple juice (warm)

Method

Corn husks need to be boiled in water for 10 minutes and then kept soaked for one hour so that they are pliable. Mix cotija cheese and cream cheese in a bowl and in another, mix lime juice and guava paste. For masa, mix masa harina, salt, baking powder, nutmeg and cinnamon in a bowl. To make the mixture crumbly, mix in 2¼ cups of hot water. With an electric mixer, beat shortening and butter till it is fluffy and light. Also, combine half of the harina mixture and sugar. Mix well while adding alternatively apple juice and the final amount of masa harina mixture. The batter should be of a thick consistency. 16 large husks which are pliable are used to make wrappers for 16 tamales. Another 32 ties need to be made in the form of strips. Now, to arrange, put ⅓ cup of Masa in the middle of each husk with a couple of lines of cheese and guava mixtures. Fold them to make the tamales and tie them with husk strips. In a steamer basket, place them over simmering water. It should take one hour before the husks would unwrap without difficulty. Cool before serving. Enjoy!

Spring Vegetable Tagine

Ingredients

1 fennel bulb sliced

8 radishes, quartered

2 cups of fava beans
1 sliced onion
1 cup of mashed garlic
¼ cup of olive oil.
1 tablespoons coriander
1 teaspoons of ginger

¼ teaspoons turmeric
¼ cup of vegetable broth
24 asparagus spears
2 cups of green peas
1 tablespoons of lemon juice
⅔ cup of almonds, sliced

Method

Mix radishes, onion, fava beans, parsley, fennel, garlic in Dutch oven. Add oil, ginger, coriander, turmeric and pepper and salt. Add broth and put it in the oven to cook for one and half hours. Stir in between. Add peas and asparagus and put back to oven. Pour in lemon juice after recipe is done, add almonds and parsley. Serve. Enjoy!

SWISS CHOCOLATE ALMOND TART

Ingredients

Crust

2 teaspoons of egg replacer powder
¼ cup of sugar
¼ teaspoons of salt
1½ teaspoons of cornstarch
1 tablespoons of margarine
½ teaspoons of vanilla extract

Filling

¼ cup almonds
1 12oz low fat milk
½ cup of coconut milk
½ cup of sugar
4 oz. of chopped chocolate

Method

For crust mix together egg replacer powder, salt, almond meal, margarine, cornstarch, vanilla and sugar and beat. Chill for 15 minutes. Make dough and sprinkle with cornstarch. Take a pie pan and press the crust equally. Bake for 8 minutes. For filling boil milk, sugar and coconut milk in a saucepan. In a bowl mix chocolate and milk and whisk until melted. Pour on the crust and bake for 10 minutes. Serve Enjoy!

AUBERGINE SCHNITZEL

Ingredients

Pesto

3 cups basil
2 tablespoons of pine nuts
2 garlic cloves
¼ cup of olive oil
1½ tablespoons of lemon juice

Schnitzel

2 red bell peppers
2 eggplants
¼ cup of olive oil
2 eggs
1 cup flour
3 tomatoes, sliced

4 oz. of cheddar

Lemon Aioli
⅔ cup of soymilk

⅓ cup of lemon juice
2 cloves mince garlic
1¼ cup of vegetable oil
½ teaspoons of salt

Method

For pesto: process nuts, basil, garlic and add lemon juice and olive oil. Pulse again. For the schnitzel: bake bell peppers. Cool and peel. Cut into 4 strips. Bake for 7 to 8 minutes. Cool and shift to plate. Oil the eggplants and grill for 2 minutes. Blend all the ingredients of Lemon Aioli. Serve Enjoy!

Vegan Lemony Linzer

Ingredients

1 cup of flour
1 cup of almond flour
¼ cup of sugar
4 oz. of Earth balance margarine
2 tablespoons of honey

2 teaspoons of lemon zest
2 teaspoons of egg replacer powder
½ teaspoons of almond extract
½ teaspoons of vanilla extract
½ cup of raspberry jam

Method

Combine both flours and sugar in bowl. Add margarine and mix. Blend honey, lemon zest, egg replacer, and water in a bowl. Add flour mixture and honey. Shape like dough and refrigerate. Cut them in heart shapes. Bake for 5-6 minutes. Allow to cool. Make hole in the cookies and pour jam into it. Serve Enjoy!

Garlic Naan

Naan is the most common flat bread that is consumed by the people residing in the Indian subcontinent. It smells fabulous when brushed with garlic oil.

Ingredients

1.25 oz. of dry yeast
3 ⅓ cups of bread flour
2 teaspoons of sugar
1 teaspoons of salt

½ cup of yoghurt
4 tablespoons of olive oil
1 clove of garlic, mashed

Method

Combine the flour, salt and sugar in a stand mixer. Dissolve yeast in warm water. Add yoghurt and olive oil into the mixture. Make dough and let it rise at a warm temperature. Pour the garlic with olive oil. Heat a medium skillet. Roll out the dough in 8 inch and shift to skillet. Cook for a minute and change the sides. Cook until both the sides are golden brown in color. Serve hot after brushing with garlic oil. Enjoy!

Spicy Chickpeas

This dish is easy to cook, filling and nutritious; it also tastes very smooth to almost everyone's liking.

Ingredients

1 liter water
400 grams chickpeas
1½ teaspoon Salt
2 teaspoons Cumin powder
1½ teaspoons kachari powder
4 Bay leaves
4 Black cardamoms
2 teaspoons Fennel powder
5 teaspoons Pomegranate powder

2 teaspoons Dried mango powder
3 teaspoons Coriander powder
1½ teaspoons Red chili powder
1 teaspoon Aromatic spice
1 teaspoon Sweet soda
12 cloves of Garlic
3 teaspoons Finely chopped green chilies
2 teaspoons Dried Fenugreek Leaves
5 teaspoons Lemon juice

Method

Put the chickpeas in the vessel. Then mix soda bi carb, large black cardamoms and bay leaves and tie up in a cloth. Leave it for 4-5 hours. Boil the wet chickpeas with salt. Blend all the spices together to make a spice rub. Pour the mixture in a bowl. Mix the chickpeas with spices. Now the food is ready to relish. Enjoy!

Soya Haleem

Haleem is a popular curry prepared during the holy month of Ramadan with meat and various lentils. This dish is a vegetarian version of the popular dish.

Ingredients

8 to 10 cloves of Garlic
1, 1 inch piece of Ginger
3 Green chilies
3 tablespoons Olive oil
2 Sliced onions
1 tablespoon Red chili powder
1 stick Cinnamon
5-6 Black peppercorns
2-3 Cardamom pods
2-3 teaspoons Cumin seeds
2-3 Bay leaves
1 cup Soy granules

3 tablespoons Green gram
3 tablespoons Red lentil
3 tablespoons Black gram
½ cup Whole wheat or cracked wheat
1 cup Vegetable stock
1 teaspoon cumin powder
1 teaspoon Coriander powder
1 teaspoon Spicy mixture
½ teaspoon Turmeric powder
A few chopped cilantro leaves
A few chopped mint leaves

Method

All the ingredients like ginger, garlic and green chilies are blended into a rough paste. Fry the onions in a hot pan till golden brown in olive oil. The red chili powder and the ginger are added. Sauté well .Now adds the green gram, soy granules and black gram. Mix well. Then add the powder spice for seasoning. Now cook thoroughly. Garnish it with lime, fresh coriander, chopped green chilies. Enjoy!

CURRY OF MANGO JUICE

This dish calls for both unripe and ripe mangoes to make a tangy, sweet curry for ideal summer. This tangy dish goes well with flat bread or rice.

Ingredients

1 cup Mango puree
1 cup Raw mango puree
1 cup Thin buttermilk
1½ teaspoons Oil
½ teaspoon Black Cumin
½ teaspoon Fenugreek Seeds

¼ cup paste of gram flour mixed with buttermilk
2-3 Green chilies slit
Salt and pepper
¼ teaspoon Asafetida
½ teaspoon Mustard seeds
Curry leaves

Method

In a bowl add the mango puree, raw mango puree and buttermilk. Add to this the gram flour paste to get rid of the lumps. Mix the red chili, cumin, curry leaves, fenugreek seeds and turmeric into a mixture. Heat the oil in a frying pan. Stir the mélange properly Add the green chilies to it and sauté. Let its simmer for about 6-8 minutes till the mixture thickens a bit. Mix into the mango mix and serve. Enjoy!

STUFFED BITTER GOURD WITH CHEESE

This dish gets rid of the bitterness of the gourd and has an exotic flavor owing to the delicious Indian spices in it.

Ingredients

4 tablespoons Olive oil
3 Medium bitter gourds
1 Medium sliced onion
½ diced yellow bell pepper
A pinch of clove powder
A pinch of red chili flakes
1 Small head of roughly chopped broccoli
½ Diced tomato
½ teaspoon Brown sugar
2½ tablespoons Corn flour
1 teaspoon Onion powder
½ teaspoon Garlic powder
5 Basil leaves
A pinch of cinnamon powder

A dash of balsamic vinegar
½ cup Emmental cheese, grated (You can use regular processed cheese too)

Spice dust / coating

2½ tablespoons Gram flour
2½ tablespoons Corn flour
1 teaspoon Cumin powder

Method

First cut the bitter gourd. Scoop out the seeds and inner flesh. Keep the bitter gourds pressed under a heavy weight to release the moisture Sprinkle them with salt. The excess water is to be drained. Heat 2 tablespoons of oil in a pan and add the onion, bell pepper, and broccoli and sauté. Other ingredients are mixed properly in a big platter. The bitter gourd is filled with grated cheese. Do shallow fry in the heat. After it gets crispy then savor it with some Indian chutney or a sauce. Enjoy!

INDIAN PEAS KEBOBS

Ingredients

1½ teaspoons Cumin
1½ tablespoons Ghee (can be found at any Indian store in your locality)
1 pinch Asafetida mixed with water
3 teaspoons Green chilies, chopped
1 teaspoon cilantro powder

Salt, to taste
2 to 3 tablespoons gram flour
2 tablespoons ginger, chopped
1 bowl, de-shelled peas
¼ teaspoon Turmeric powder

Method

In a pan, add the cumin seeds, asafetida water, ghee, green chilies and ginger and mix. Sauté the ingredients for about 30 seconds. Mix gram flour to it and make a stiff mixture. Mash the peas and add to this mix. Shape into small rounds and shallow fry until brown from both sides. Serve hot. Enjoy!

CORN KEBOBS

Ingredients

2 cups Corn kernels
½ cup potato, boiled and grated
½ teaspoon black pepper powder
½ teaspoon garam masala (can be found in your local Indian store)
2 tablespoons Grated cheddar cheese
−2 Chopped green chilies

2 teaspoons Chopped ginger
½ teaspoon White pepper powder
1 Pinch mace powder
Few fresh mint leaves
Salt to taste
3-4 teaspoons Refined oil

Method

First grate the corn. Then all the elements are added and mix properly. To make barrel shaped kebobs cut the mixture into equal portion. In a non - sticky frying pan the oil is heated. Keep frying the kebabs until the color is golden. Serve hot garnished with some mint leaves and a side of tomato ketchup. Enjoy!

STUFFED SPICY MUSHROOMS

Ingredients

1 teaspoon Oil
2 teaspoons Butter
1 teaspoon Cumin
1 Chopped red chili
1 large Chopped onion
1 teaspoon Chopped garlic
1 teaspoon Red chili powder
1 teaspoon Coriander seeds

Salt, to taste
Water, to deglaze
1 Chopped tomato
1 cup Corn kernels
A pinch of sugar
10 Chopped mushroom stalks
Chopped Parsley

Method

1 teaspoon oil and 2 teaspoon butter are combined in a sauce pan. Red chili powder, coriander, cumin, onions, salt are mixed and sautéed. Then add a pinch of sugar and tomato to keep it tangy. Cook till the mushrooms release some water. Then corn and chopped parsley are added to the mixture and cooked until tender. Serve hot. Enjoy!

SPICED VEGETABLE RICE

This dish is comfort food at its best!

Ingredients

1 cup Rice
2 Carrots
10 Beans
2 Potatoes
Salt to taste
Water as needed
½ cup Fresh peas
1 tablespoon Mustard oil
2 teaspoons Cumin seeds

2 teaspoons Garlic paste
½ cup Fenugreek leaves
½ cup Yoghurt
2 teaspoon Yellow chili powder
8 to 10 Green chilies, sliced
3 teaspoons Ginger, sliced
1 teaspoon Green cardamom powder
1 teaspoon Mace powder
½ cup Fresh cream

Method

Heat mustard oil in a vessel; add cumin seeds, fenugreek leaves, garlic paste and sauté. Boil water in a pan, add salt and blanch potatoes, carrots, peas and beans, separately for 2-3 minutes. Once they are boiled, rinse them in cold water. For 20 minutes soak the rice. Add water yoghurt, vegetables and salt yellow chili powder, turmeric powder in a bowl and gently stir .Once the rice is cooked add the cream and sauté. Combine all the components in a large vessel and heat for a while. Serve hot. Enjoy!

Whole Wheat Pasta in Mushroom Sauce

This pasta is a healthier vegan choice of lunch food. Any mushroom lover can definitely gorge on it.

Ingredients

½ cup Shitake mushroom-soaked in warm water for 15 minutes

1 tablespoon Fresh thyme or fresh chopped parsley

2 tablespoons White wine

100 grams Whole wheat pasta-penne or linguine

½ cup Fresh sliced mushroom

1 tablespoon Chopped onion

1 clove of Garlic

Pepper and Salt for taste

Method

Put the pasta in boiling salted water. Whilst the pasta is boiling, prepare the sauce. Sauté the onion and garlic in olive oil, the add mushroom and wine in a heavy bottomed pan. Some of the water, in which shitake mushroom was drenched, should be poured into it. While the wine is evaporated, herbs and salt should be added. Pour the sauce over the pasta and serve immediately! Enjoy!

Fried Potato and Cottage Cheese Cubes

The perfect party starter – crispy, spicy and delicious!

Ingredients

2 Parboiled potatoes

250 gram Cottage cheese

Oil to flash fry (Flash fry is a process in which the potatoes/cottage cheese are immersed in hot oil and fried for 3-4 minutes or till colored on the outside

1+1 teaspoons Turmeric

Salt, to taste

1+1tsp Red chili powder

1 to 2 teaspoons Oil

Method

The par boiled potatoes should be marinated with half the turmeric, salt, chili powder and some oil in a bowl. Flash fry them. Keep aside. In another bowl, the other components like the cottage cheese cubes with turmeric, salt, some oil, and chili powder are combined. Let marinate for about 10 minutes and flash fry them. Combine the potatoes and cottage cheese and thread them on toothpicks and serve with a side of salad. Enjoy!

Tamarind Rice

Ingredients

1 cup Rice-cooked 'bite-like'

2 tablespoons Ghee

1 Sprig curry leaves
2 -3 Whole red chilies
1 teaspoon Asafetida
1 teaspoon Mustard seeds
1 tablespoon Split Bengal Gram
1 tablespoon Skinned Black Gram

2 teaspoons salt
Peanuts, optional
½ cup tamarind pulp
1 teaspoon chili powder
2 teaspoons sugar

Method

Heat ghee, curry leaves, whole red chilies, asafetida, mustard should be combined with the Bengal gram and black gram. Add the rice and sauté till well mixed. Dilute the tamarind pulp with water until it becomes 1 cup and add to the rice. Sauté till the rice gets colored. Bring to a boil. Then add the rest of ingredients. Simmer for some time and serve. Enjoy!

CUMIN SPICED VEGETABLES

Ingredients

2 tablespoons Butter
2 tablespoons Olive oil
2 teaspoons Cumin
1 tablespoon Red chili powder
1 cup Pureed spinach
8-9 Baby potatoes
5-6 Baby carrots

1 teaspoon Ginger garlic chili paste
2 teaspoons Lemon juice
2 Onions
Salt & pepper to taste
Cilantro leaves, to garnish
A pinch of Green Cardamom powder

Method

Butter and oil are poured in a pan. Cumin, ginger garlic paste, carrots and potato all ingredients are combined and put them in the pan. Cook for some time and add the seasoning and cilantro leaves. Cook for a while and add in the spinach puree to it. Mix well and scatter with a drops of cream. Now serve hot. Enjoy!

SOUTHERN STYLE OKRA

Ingredients

Refined oil
250 grams Okra or lady finger
1 teaspoon Mustard seeds
1 teaspoon Fenugreek seeds
1 Chopped onion
2 cloves Garlic chopped garlic
2 Green chilies slit
A pinch of turmeric powder

A pinch of Red chili powder
1 teaspoon Coriander powder
Water, as needed
3 teaspoons Tamarind extract
10 grams Chopped Palm sugar
Cilantro leaves, to garnish
Grated coconut, to garnish
Salt to taste

Method

Heat the oil in a frying pan. Add the okra, fenugreek seeds, mustard seeds then season it with salt and let it fry. Heat another pan. Combine onion, garlic and green chilies to the pan and sauté. Add tamarind extract & palm sugar. To create the steam, sprinkle with water. Cook for 7-8 minutes. It is accomplished with some grated coconut. Enjoy!

Mediterranean Watermelon Salad

The hydrating components of it always make you feel fresh. This nutritious salad is ideal for breakfast.

Ingredients

1 bowl Watermelon cubes
2 Yellow bell peppers
1 cup Onions
1 cup Cucumber
1 cup Tomatoes
1 cup Pomegranate Juice
1 tablespoon Mustard paste
2 tablespoons Olive oil
1 head Romaine lettuce

4-5 Rocket lettuce
1 teaspoon Flax seeds
A pinch of cumin powder
A pinch of Oregano
Salt & pepper
10-12 Olives
1 teaspoon Parsley chopped
Pistachios, for garnish

Method

Pour pomegranate juice into a bowl. Mustard paste, cumin powder, oregano, salt & pepper are added to it and whisk in the olive oil. In another bowl, the watermelon cubes, onions, cucumber and yellow bell peppers are combined. Mix them all well. Add lettuce leaves, flax seeds and pistachios to the watermelon mixture. Serve chilled. Enjoy!

Indian Stir Fry

Spicy Indian dish, ideal for cold winter evenings!

Ingredients

Cumin seed powder-1 teaspoon
Turmeric powder-1 teaspoon
Red chili powder-2 teaspoon
Coriander powder-1 tablespoon
Chopped onion-1 large
Tomato puree-1 cup
Cumin seed powder-1 teaspoon
Turmeric powder-1 teaspoon
Red chili powder-2 teaspoon
Coriander powder-1 tablespoon
Salt, to taste

Baby corns-1 cup
Button mushrooms-8 to 9
Red pepper-½
Coriander seeds-3 tablespoons
Peppercorn seeds-3tbsp
yellow pepper-½
Canned chopped artichoke-1
Fresh chopped coriander leaves-2tbsp

Method

The baby corn is shredded. The stem of the mushrooms are peeled off and chop into quarters. Cut the artichokes. Put the baby corn in a pan, but do not cook too much. Add the peppercorn and coriander seeds to a pan. Repeat with mushrooms and peppers. As the canned artichokes are pre-cooked, they need not be blanched. In a mortar pestle add the spices and ground until they are powdered. Roast to get the right aroma. Mix all the veggies with the roasted spices and slow cook on a low flame. Serve hot! Enjoy!

INDIAN STYLE COTTAGE CHEESE

Ingredients

Cottage cheese, cut into rectangles - 250gm
Chopped tomatoes - 6
Cashew Nuts-15
Crushed garlic -5 cloves
Butter-2 tablespoons
Fenugreek Leaves - 2 tablespoons

Sugar-1 teaspoons
Cream (Optional)
Cinnamon stick-1"
Salt, to taste
Red chili powder, to taste
Milk-2 to 3 tablespoons

Method

Put 1 tablespoon butter in a pan. Once it melts, add the garlic, cinnamon and cashews and combine. Fry, till the color changes. Add the tomatoes and sauté till the tomatoes become soft and add chili powder & salt .Take another pan to grill the cottage cheese pieces. In the same pan add the tomato-cashew paste. Remove the cottage cheese pieces. Now add the fenugreek leaves, cinnamon and sugar to it. Let it simmer for 1 minute. Top it with cream. Dish out immediately! Enjoy!

VGV VEGETABLE SANDWICH

Ingredients

3 Green, red and yellow bell peppers
1 Onion
1 Leak
1 Yellow squash
1 Zucchini

1 Broccoli, cut into florets
A few lettuce leaves
Salt and pepper to season
3 tablespoons Olive oil
4 slices Bread

Method

Grill the bell peppers, squash and zucchini on both sides after basting them with olive oil. Two slices of bread are grilled. Then they are spiced with pepper and salt. Layer a few leaves of lettuce and add the vegetable mix. Now dig in with chips. Enjoy!

POMMES GRATIN

Ingredients

Butter - 2 teaspoons
Cream – 1 cup
Thyme - 1 teaspoon
Bashed garlic - 2 cloves
Peeled and thinly sliced potatoes -3

Grated cheese (Cheddar or Gruyere) – 5 tablespoons
Salt, to taste
Pepper, to taste
A pinch of Nutmeg powder

Method

First you add 2 teaspoons butter with 1 cup cream in a pan. Let the cream reduce a little. Add thyme, sliced potatoes garlic, salt, pepper and nutmeg with 3 tablespoons cheese. The creamy potatoes are transferred in a greased baking dish. Top with the rest of the cheese and butter till the cheese is melted, bake it. Finally it is ready to dig in. Enjoy!

RAVA DOSA

A delicious traditional South Indian breakfast food: crispy, thin and light – ideal for those looking for a light breakfast.

Ingredients

Fine semolina -1 cup
Rice flour or plain flour -½ cup
Oil-1 tablespoon
Soda bi carb -1/8 teaspoon

Buttermilk -2 ½ cups
Finely chopped coriander -1 teaspoon
Green chilies chopped fine - 2

Method

Blend all the ingredients together. More buttermilk needs to be added if necessary. Sprinkle some water in the batter. Heat griddle to very hot. Lower the heat and pour the batter on it in circular motions. When the smoke begins to rise pour some oil (½ teaspoon) over dosa, and trail some around it. Roll it in a three-fold cylinder. Serve hot with onion. Enjoy!

POHA

This delicious flat rice dish is ideal for a light evening snack.

Ingredients

Flat rice-1 Cup
Oil -1tbsp
Asafetida-1/8 teaspoon
Mustard seeds-1 teaspoon

Onions-chopped fine-½ cup
Curry leaves -8 to 10
Whole red chilies -2 to 3
Small diced potatoes-½ cup

Turmeric -½ teaspoon
Salt or to taste-2 teaspoon
Nicely chopped green chillies-1 teaspoons

Lemon juice -1 tablespoon
Chopped coriander leaves -1 tablespoon
Lemon wedges for garnish

Method

Wash the flat rice and leave it in the colander to drain out completely. Mustard seeds, asafetida, onions are poured into the heated oil. Increase the heat. Add the flat rice and salt into the mixture. Sauté till it is mixed and heated through. Combine lemon juice, chilies and half coriander. Garnish with the rest of the coriander after transfer on to a serving bowl. Enjoy!

SPICED SPROUTS

Ingredients

Green gram sprouts -200gm
Ghee -2 tablespoon
Cumin seeds -1 tablespoons
Finely chopped garlic-1 tablespoons
Salt -2 tablespoon
Chili powder -½ teaspoon
Turmeric -½ tablespoon

Yogurt-beaten smooth-½ cup
Finely shredded ginger -1 tablespoon
Tomatoes-grated (optional) -½ cup
Garam masala -½ tablespoon (can be found in any Indian store in your locality)
Powdered coriander seeds -2 tablespoons
Chopped coriander leaves-1 tablespoon

Method

Heat the ghee. The cumin, garlic and ginger, tomatoes are combined and added to the hot ghee. Stir fry till the fat separates. Then salt, turmeric, garam masala are added to it. Then add the sprouts and stirring a few times. Bring the mixture to a boil. Add 1 cup of water and yogurt. Simmer uncovered for about a minute. Serve hot. Enjoy!

SUJI DHOKLA

This is calorie free item. This traditional West Indian dish is a favorite of kids due to its spongy texture.

Ingredients

Semolina- 1 cup
Ginger paste -½ teaspoon
Green chili paste -½ teaspoon
Salt -1 teaspoon
Oil -1 tablespoon
Sour curd-½ cup

Water-½ cup
Fruit salt or baking soda-1 teaspoon
Curry leaves – 3
Mustard seeds - 1 teaspoon
Slit green chilies - 2

Method

Mix the semolina, ginger paste, chili paste, fruit salt, sugar and oil and beat in the curd. Then the mixture is poured into the greased vessel and placed in a steamer for 5 minutes. The oil is heated then, add curry leaves, mustard seeds and green chilies. Sauté till the mustard stops popping and pour over the prepared dhokla. Cut the dhokla into desired size pieces. Let it cool and remove from the vessel once cool. Serve with a mint dip. Enjoy!

Split Bengal Gram Dhokla

Ingredients

Split Bengal gram-250 grams
Yoghurt- ½ cup
Sugar, to taste
Oil- 2 tablespoons
Mustard seeds-1 teaspoon

Salt to taste
Water- 2 tablespoons
Lemon juice- 1 teaspoon
Red chillies-3
Asafetida- 1 pinch

Method

Soak the split Bengal gram in water for at least 2 hours and blend with the yoghurt, to form the consistency of pancake batter. Mix in the sugar and leave in a warm place. A mold is greased and put in a steamer. The soda bi carb is added to the batter. Mix well till light and fluffy. Immediately pour into the prepared vessel. Steam. Remove, cool and cut into cubes. Pour the mustard seeds over dhokla cubes. Garnish by dripping grated coconut and coriander leaves. Enjoy!

Rice Dhokla

This delicious dish aids in digestion.

Ingredients

Rice flour -200 grams
Semolina – ½ cup
Yogurt -½ cup
Sugar to taste
Oil -4 teaspoons
Mustard seeds-½ teaspoons
Whole red peppers -1 to 2

Lemon juice -1 teaspoon
A pinch of asafetida powder
Water as required
Salt to taste
Greased metal plates for cooking the dhokla-2,6"

Method

The rice flour, semolina, sugar, yogurt and rice flour are combined and 1 teaspoon oil into a smooth paste. Add the lemon juice, water and asafetida. Keep the steamer over the stove for the water to boil. Make a batter of dropping consistency. Heat oil in a pan and add the mustard seeds, add 2 tablespoons water when the color darkens. Put batter into prepared plates and steam. Pour the mustard seed mix over the dhokla cubes. Enjoy!

MICROWAVE DHOKLA

Delicious, quick to make and highly nutritious!

Ingredients

Gram flour-1 cup
Ginger paste-1 teaspoon
Green chili paste-1 teaspoon
Turmeric-1 teaspoon
Salt-1 teaspoon
Sugar-1 teaspoon

Oil-1 tablespoon
Sour curd-1 cup
Water-1 cup
Fruit salt-1 teaspoon
Curry leaves-3
Mustard seeds-1 teaspoon

Method

Chili paste, salt, turmeric, the gram flour, ginger paste, sugar and oil are mixed together and beat in the curds till smooth. Add the fruit salt, stir gently and pour immediately into the greased microwavable dish, cover and cook at HI for 6-8 minutes, rotating the dish once. Heat the oil for the tempering; add the mustard seeds, curry leaves and green chilies and add 1 cup water. Sauté till it is slightly colored. Pour over the dhokla and cut into desired sized pieces. Garnish with the coconut and cilantro. Serve at room temperature. Enjoy!

BARNYARD MILLET DHOKLA

Ingredients

Barnyard Millet-¾ cup
Sour yogurt-1 cup
Ginger paste-1tsp
Green chilies paste to taste
Rock salt-1 teaspoons
Dry red peppers-2 whole

Curry leaves-6 to 7
Cumin seeds-1 teaspoon
Oil/ghee-2 teaspoons
Grated coconut and fresh coriander for garnish

Method

The barnyard millet is roasted in a pan very lightly and do not let it brown. Prepare the batter by mixing the millet, chili paste, rock salt, ginger paste and yoghurt. Leave the mixture to ferment overnight. Place a tin into the steamer and heat for 20 minutes. Grease a tin with little ghee and transfer the batter into it. Let it cool and heat up some oil and temper the cumin seeds and curry leaves in it. Add some water to it and pour over the dhokla Serve topped with some grated coconut and coriander. Enjoy!

Mix Vegetables and Cheese Skewers

This is very child friendly evening recipe, ideal for kids' parties.

Ingredients

Garlic -5 cloves
Cumin-½ teaspoon
Pepper, to taste
Cottage cheese-250 grams
Cucumber-1
Squeezed lemon -1
Green olives-10

Chili flakes-½ teaspoon
Black pepper-½ teaspoon
Handful of basil leaves
Red wine vinegar-1tbsp
Nicely cut zucchini-½
Red bell pepper-1

Method

In the grinder add garlic, green olives, chili flakes, cumin, black pepper, few sprigs of basil leaves and salt. Add olive oil, red wine vinegar, and lemon juice, and then mix it with the paste. Grind it all together. Cube the onion, cottage cheese, red bell pepper, zucchini and dunk into the marinade. Thread on to the skewers. Place the skewers on a pre-heated the grill pan and sprinkle it with olive oil. Continuously turn until all sides have browned. Serve hot. Enjoy!

Vegetable Au Gratin

Ingredients

Snap Beans blanched and-chopped -½ cup
Diced cauliflower-1 head
Mushrooms-sliced thin -½ cup
Oil -2 teaspoon
Cumin seeds -1 teaspoon

Ground black pepper -¼ teaspoons
Roasted All-purpose flour- 3 tablespoons
Milk -2 cups
Finely chopped onions-¼ cup
Salt or to taste-1 teaspoon
Grated cheese-1 cup

Method

Gradually pour the milk into the flour (to avoid lumps), bring to a boil and simmer for a minute. Turn of the heat and add the cheese to it. Keep aside. The oil is heated, add the cumin seeds. When it splutters, add the onions, mushrooms and vegetables and stir-fry over high heat, till well covered with oil and vegetables are half cooked. Pour the cheese sauce over the mixed veggies and serve immediately. Enjoy!

Stuffed Mushroom Caps with Cheese

Ingredients

Button mushrooms-200 grams

Medium diced onion -1

Bell pepper diced-⅓
Olive oil-1 tablespoon
Few sprigs thyme
Leaf sage-1
Mozzarella cheese-2 tablespoons
bell pepper diced-⅓
Garlic-2 cloves

Pinch of pepper and salt
Balsamic vinegar-½ tablespoon
Gorgonzola cheese-2 tablespoons
White wine (optional)
Diced dates-2 tablespoons
Vegetable stock to deglaze

Method

Marinate the mushrooms with balsamic vinegar, thyme, sage salt, and olive oil .Deglaze the pan with water/stock or white wine .the diced onion, bell pepper and garlic are sweated, while the mushroom are marinating. Add the diced dates. Then season to taste. Give some time to cool the mixture. Add the mozzarella and gorgonzola to complete the filling for the mushroom stuffing. Your dish is ready to eat. Enjoy!

 YOGURT KEBAB

Ingredients

Yogurt-2 cups
Cottage cheese-100 grams
Finely chopped almonds-10
Chopped raisins -7 to 8
White pepper powder-½ teaspoon
Chopped onion-2 teaspoons

Chopped ginger-1 teaspoon
Green cardamom powder-½ teaspoon
Oil -to grill
Salt- to taste
Corn flour- to taste

Method

In a muslin cloth yogurt is hanged overnight. Then ginger and onion in minimum oil are sautéed. Add crumbled cottage cheese, cardamom, salt, chopped raisins, coriander, almonds, and the onion mixture. Take the yoghurt in a bowl. Now, make round patties with this gooey mix. Grease a pan with olive oil .Till they turn brown, grill these. Now serve hot with chutney. Enjoy!

GREEN CURRY PORRIDGE

Ingredients

2 tablespoons of olive oil
2 tablespoons of lemongrass
3 garlic cloves
1 tablespoon of coriander
1 ¾ cups of brown rice
4 teaspoons of sea salt
1 14-ounce of can coconut milk

1 Serano Chile
1 tablespoon of ginger
1 cup of cilantro
½ cup of green onion
1 cup of sorrel

Direction

Take pot add olive oil, lemongrass, coriander, garlic, and rice. Stir until rice kernels are fragrant. Add water and stir 2 teaspoons of salt and let soup simmer gently. In meantime, mix coconut milk, Serrano Chile, ginger, cilantro, sorrel, green onion tops, and remaining 2 teaspoons of salt in a blender. Add coconut milk mixture to porridge. Simmer for 10-15 minutes, or until squash is warm. Taste for seasoning and top with green onion, chopped cilantro, olive oil, and lime. Enjoy!

SAKE MUSHROOMS

Ingredients

1 cup- rice flour
½ teaspoon- sea salt
8 ounces- mushrooms
1 cup -sake
1 tablespoon - virgin olive

1 tablespoon - unsalted butter

Miso Butter

1 tablespoon -butter
2 teaspoons- miso
1 teaspoon- sesame seeds

Direction

First Combine rice flour and salt in bowl. Then you have to dip mushroom slice in rice flour, Repeat till mushrooms are covered. Then in skillet heat olive oil and butter, and place mushrooms until it is deeply golden. While mushrooms are cooking then make miso butter by mixing butter, miso and sesame seeds in bowl. Mix till uniform and serve mushrooms with Miso butter. It has great taste and it is loved all aged group of people. Enjoy!

GUACAMOLE

Ingredients

1 medium size of garlic clove
½ teaspoon of salt
4 ripe- avocados
½ medium size white onion

A squeeze of lime juice
For serving: chive blossoms and chopped cilantro

Method

First step is to sprinkle garlic with salt and chop finely. Then you use spoon to remove avocado flesh into bowl. And then sprinkle avocado with onions and garlic, and then use large fork for folding everything together. You may like chunky guacamole, so fold, chop with edge of fork. After folding add lime juice, and mix some more. Taste and then you can adjust with salt or lime juice, and serve topped with cilantro and chives. Enjoy!

Kale Rice Bowl

Ingredients

Clarified butter or olive oil
1 bunch kale, de-stemmed, chopped/
shredded
3 cups of cooked brown rice

Egg
Salted Greek yogurt
Big drizzle of virgin olive oil
Za'atar
Sesame seeds

To serve
Capers dried, and fried blistered in butter

Method

First take large skillet and heat olive oil on medium heat then you can add kale and pinch of the salt and sauté until the kale is softens a bit and brightens, for a minute. Then you have to stir in rice and cook till the rice is hot and if rice is on dry side add some water. Now it's time to serve kale rice with the topping of poached eggs, capers, olive oil with yogurt drizzle and plenty of Zaatar. Enjoy!

Raised Broccoli with Orange and Parmesan

Ingredients

½ cup orange juice
1 14-ounce can crushed tomatoes
1 broccoli head florets
¼ teaspoon of fresh oregano
¼ teaspoon of pepper flakes

¼ teaspoon of sea salt
⅛ teaspoon of black pepper
1 tablespoon of olive oil
¼ cup Parmesan cheese
2 tablespoons of toasted almonds

Directions

First you have to take saucepan on the medium heat then blend tomatoes and the orange juice then let it to boil. Stir in the broccoli. Then you have to put red pepper flakes and cook till broccoli is just tender for few minutes. Season with pepper and salt and other spices. Transfer to the serving bowl. Enjoy!

Fennel Mushrooms

Ingredients

12 ounces of mushrooms
1 tablespoon of unsalted butter
Few pinches grain sea salt
1 bulb of fennel
1-2 tablespoons of crème fraiche
2 tablespoons of fresh dill

Bunch of chives
Ground black pepper
Bunch of sorrel watercress, or arugula
1 teaspoon olive oil

Directions

First step is to cut the mushrooms and then take large skillet and melt the butter. Then you add mushroom and pinch of salt and then use spatula stir till it is coated. And then you have to sauté for 4-5minute when the mushroom is done stir in fennel. When you have finished the cooking remove it from the heat and then put crème fraiche. Then add chives and dill, salt and more pepper. Serve hot! Enjoy!

Tomato Tarte Tatin Recipe

Ingredients

2 yellow onions
2 tablespoons of olive oil, clarified butter
24 oz. tomatoes
½ teaspoon of sea salt

2 teaspoons of balsamic vinegar
1 tablespoon of flour
One lemon
1 pie of crust

Directions

First you have to preheat the oven to 205 C. While the oven is warming up, you have to heat a skillet on medium flame and then you can sauté onion and pinch of salt in butter. Cook the onion and caramelize for 10-15 minutes and then remove it from heat. Then add tomatoes and put some flour and now you can sprinkle mixture with salt and lemon. Roll pie dough and cover it with the mixture and bake in oven till golden brown. Cool before cutting into pieces. Serve warm. Enjoy!

Breakfast Polenta Recipe

Ingredients

4 cups of water
½ teaspoon of salt
1 cup polenta
½ cup of almonds, toasted

½ cup of dried fruit
Honey
Cream

Directions

First you have to bring water to a boil and then put salt and polenta stir it and reduce the heat. Simmer for 30 minutes and if the polenta gets thick and it is dry, just pour in some water. If you want tenderer polenta then you can cook for longer time. The polenta is ready to serve. Spoon the warm dish in bowl and serve topped with dry fruit, almond, cream and the drizzle of honey. Polenta is quite healthy option and it is ideal for breakfast and then what you are waiting for. Enjoy!

$\mathcal{A}$ TASTY FRITTATA RECIPE

Ingredients

1 tablespoon - olive oil
1 cup- gram flour
1 -yellow onion, chopped
3 - Potatoes

½ cup- yellow zucchini
¼ cup- goat cheese
¼ cup- pumpkin seeds
Salt

Direction

First you have to preheat the oven and then take bowl and add the gram flour and pour in some water in it to make a thick paste. Add some salt to it. Then you have to take skillet add olive oil, salt and onion and sauté it till the onion is brown for 5 minutes. Then add zucchini and potatoes and you have to cook for another 3 minutes and turn heat down then add gram flour mix over low heat. Add the cilantro, chili sauce and sprinkle onion potato mixture on top. Bake the oven for 9 minutes add crumble of goat cheese and pumpkin seeds over frittata and serve it. Enjoy!

$\mathcal{L}$ ORI'S SKILLET SMASHED POTATO RECIPE

Ingredients

1 bag of small potatoes
Pepper and salt

1 - 2 tablespoons of olive oil

Direction

Start by peeling the potatoes and placing them in large saucepan and add salt with water. Bring water to a boil over medium heat and it is vital not to over boil. Drain the potatoes and freeze. Heat large skillet over high heat and place the potatoes in the skillet. Season with pepper and salt and cook till they are crispy. Sprinkle with fresh herbs, chives. Enjoy!

$\mathcal{R}$ OAST BANANA-PUMPKIN BREAKFAST BREAD RECIPE

Ingredients

¾ cup of golden raisins
2 ripe- bananas
2 cups of cake flour
2 teaspoons of baking powder
½ teaspoon of baking soda
6 tablespoons of unsalted butter
⅔ cup of sugar
2 tablespoons egg replacer

½ cup of coconut milk
1 teaspoons of vanilla
½ cup of pumpkin seeds

Direction

First preheat the oven to 325 degrees F and take saucepan and mix rum and raisins. Place banana on cookie sheet bake it. Now you have to sieve baking powder, flour, soda and salt together and add the egg replacer and blend with blender. Squeeze flesh of bananas in bowl, and add the coconut milk and vanilla and then blend all ingredients. Now fold pumpkin seed and raisin into batter and grease it in loaf pan and bake it in the preheated oven. Enjoy!

NETTLE PASTA

Ingredients

6 - 8 ounces of nettles
8 ounces of pasta
Olive oil
1 clove garlic
Toasted almonds

3 tablespoons sesame seeds
Onion sprouts
Cheese
Sea salt

Direction

Take pot of water and boil with salt and add nettles for 20 seconds. Then clean with cold water and chop the leaves. Then you can boil pasta and drain it. Take a pan on medium heat add olive oil, garlic and let simmer then add pasta and nettles. Now stir well and add sesame seeds and almonds. Taste it if more salt is required and then remove from heat serve family with style, topped feta with sesame seeds, sprouts, almond oil with olive oil. Enjoy!

SPRING PASTA RECIPE

Ingredients

8 ounces of pasta
Sea salt
1 tablespoon of olive oil
1 tablespoon of unsalted butter

3 big sliced asparagus, or pea shoots
Tiny broccoli trees, to serve
Chopped avocado, to serve
Chopped herbs, to serve

Directions

Melt butter on high heat and add broccoli or asparagus add a pinch of salt and cover for minute till the vegetables are brown. Add in the chopped greens and mix well. Stir till it is tender and now add pasta and toss well once pasta is hot. Now taste it and add required seasoning to it and add the avocado and reserved vegetables to it. Enjoy!

STUFFED SHELLS RECIPE

Ingredients
1 lemon

Sauce
½ cup olive oil
1½ teaspoons of pepper flakes
¾ teaspoon of sea salt

4 cloves garlic
1 28-ounce can red tomatoes

Filling
1 15-ounce ricotta cheese
¼ teaspoon of grain sea salt
5 oz. mozzarella

1 bunch chives
25-30 jumbo pasta shells

Directions

To make the sauce, combine the red pepper, salt, olive oil and garlic and heat saucepan. Put tomatoes in it and let them simmer. Once cooked, cool them. For filling mix the ricotta, salt and stir mozzarella with lemon and chives. Cook the pasta shells and fill with filling. Take a pan and pour some sauce and after that place pasta shells and then pour remaining. Cover with foil and bake for 30 minutes and then sprinkle with chives and serve hot. Enjoy!

NEW YEAR NOODLE SOUP

Ingredients
2 tablespoons of olive oil
1 onion
1 red chili
½ teaspoon of ground turmeric
1 teaspoon cumin
¼ teaspoon black pepper
1½ cups chickpeas

350 g borlotti beans
Sea salt
120 g noodles
100 g spinach leaves
½ cup cilantro leaves
2 tablespoons dill
One lime

Directions

Heat oil in pan add onion, chili,spice, split peas, salt and put the noodles with water and let it boil. Now, heat olive oil, butter, salt, onion and caramelize it. Now, put spinach, dill and cilantro and lime in the noodle pot and cook it properly. Now taste and adjust seasoning as per your likes. Serve hot! Enjoy!

Brown Butter Tortelli

Ingredients

1 packet tortelli pasta
4 tablespoons of unsalted butter
1 tablespoon balsamic vinegar
sea salt

1 lemon, grated
2 – 3 big arugula leaves
grated fresh Parmesan cheese, to serve

Direction

Keep large pot of water to boil and cook tortelli and then drain it. Put butter in skillet and then whisk butter in vinegar with lemon and salt. Add the cooked pasta to the pan of butter and toss it again. Then add the arugula and top with lemon and cheese. Serve in bowl and if you want to add seasoning Enjoy!

Pappardelle with Spiced Butter

Ingredients

¼ teaspoon of saffron threads
100 g butter
6 shallots
½ teaspoon of ginger
½ teaspoon of paprika
½ teaspoon of coriander

½ teaspoon of cinnamon
¼ teaspoon of chili flakes
225 g pappardelle pasta
225 g asparagus
60 g pine nuts
2 tablespoons parsley

Direction

Crush saffron and salt. In a frying pan put butter and cook shallots and add in all the spices and remove from heat. Take pot full of water and cook pasta and asparagus and then mix saffron and salt. Pour spiced butter over pasta and cream then toss well. Serve pasta in large bowl and sprinkle herbs and pine nuts. Enjoy!

Ginger-Poached Noodles Recipe

Ingredients

4 cups of vegetable broth
2 ounces of fresh ginger
8 ounces of firm tofu
1-2 cups of broccoli
4 ounces of spinach noodles
1 - 2 tablespoons of soy sauce
¼ cup of fresh basil

¼ cup of mint
Lime juice
Red pepper flakes
Sesame oil

Directions

Place the broth, tofu and ginger in saucepan and let it to boil and gently simmer for 10 minutes. Remove tofu from pan and then add broccoli then cook for few more minutes and then remove from pan. Add pasta, tofu and broccoli to a pot. Put the soya sauce, lemon, and basil, mint red pepper and season it sesame oil. Serve hot! Enjoy!

WALNUT MISO NOODLE RECIPE

Ingredients

4 ounces of wheat spaghetti
1 bunch of asparagus
½ cup of walnuts
¼ cup of olive oil

1 clove garlic
2 tablespoons of white miso paste
2 tablespoons of vinegar white wine
1 teaspoon of honey

Direction

Cook the pasta and toss with walnut miso dressing. For the dressing make the puree of walnut, garlic, olive oil, vinegar, honey and miso paste. (It should feel like heavy cream.) Add salt and add some more dressing to the noodles and toss well. Toss the noodles with green onion, chard stems, toasted walnut, salt and the olive oil. Spoon the noodles into a serving bowl and adjust the seasoning as needed. Enjoy!

CHEESELESS PASTA CASSEROLE RECIPE

Ingredients

1 lemon
8 ounces of whole wheat pasta
1½ cups of butternut squash
3 handfuls of kale
2 cups of Greek yogurt
3 garlic cloves

½ teaspoon sea salt
⅔ cup of sliced almonds
¼ cup of Kalamata olives
¼ cup of feta cheese
¼ cup of fresh mint

Direction

Preheat the oven to 400 degrees F and oil a baking dish and sprinkle with lemon. Boil the pasta and pour it on the butternut squash and kale. Now, drain pasta and then whisk the garlic, yogurt and salt in bowl. Add the pasta squash kale mixture to the mixture of yogurt and pour half the almonds in it. Sprinkle all this with olive oil and feta and bake it for 25 minutes. Remove from the oven and serve with fresh mint and almonds. Enjoy!

Matchstick Pasta Recipe

Ingredients

8 ounces of grain linguine or spaghetti
⅔ cup of pistachios
1 clove garlic
¼ teaspoon sea salt

¼ cup olive oil
1 large kale
1 pomegranate

Direction

First, boil the pasta and make pistachio sauce by making a puree of salt, garlic, pistachios, olive oil and set it aside. Then, add the kale to the pasta and in frying pan pour the sauce and pasta, and kale and toss it gently with pomegranate seed and salt. Now, spoon the pasta onto a platter lined with the leaves of kale and now you can sprinkle the pomegranate seeds and pistachios on the top. If you want, you can add more sauce for seasoning and enhance taste of the pasta. Enjoy!

Broccoli Pesto & Fusilli Pasta Recipe

Ingredients

1 head of broccoli
½ cup of toasted walnuts
⅓ cup of Parmesan
1 clove garlic
½ lemon juice

¼ teaspoon sea salt
⅓ cup olive oil
½ pound whole wheat pasta
3 handfuls spinach
Black olives

Directions

Take two pots, one for boiling pasta and another for broccoli. After boiling, drain and wash with cold water. Then with few broccoli trees, garlic, Parmesan, lemon juice, walnut and salt make a puree with in a food processor. Then, pour the olive oil in the food processor while blending, salt and lemon juice also if needed. Stir pasta with spinach and pesto also. Serve with the topping of broccoli florets and olives. Enjoy!

Harissa Spaghettini Recipe

Ingredients

3 cloves garlic
Sea salt
¼ cup olive oil
2 tablespoons of harissa
8 ounces of wheat spaghettini

1 bunch kale
½ cup of black olives
½ cup of pine nuts
1 lemon

Direction

First, boil pasta with salt and in meantime cut garlic and sprinkle salt and mix it to make paste. Whisk the harrisa, olive oil and garlic paste together. Before pasta is completely done, add kale to pasta water, drain and set aside. Now, heat the half of the harissa dressing in pasta pot and add kale, pasta, pine nuts, and black olives, lemon zest and pine nuts to it. Cook for a few minutes and serve remaining with harissa olive oil. Enjoy!

Big Slurp Dumpling Soup Recipe

Soups are hearty, nutritious and diet friendly – the three things every diet conscious individual craves!

Ingredients

Extra virgin olive oil
1 onion
1 vegetable bouillon
4 cups of water
Sea salt

4 cups of yellow split peas
¼ cup of fresh herbs
16 dumplings
¼ cup parmesan cheese grated

Directions

Take large pot of water for cooking of dumplings. At same time add onion, olive oil, bouillon to a skillet and cook on medium heat. Cook for a few minute till the onion softens. Add water and let it simmer. Add the seasoning to the broth as per your taste. Add the yellow peas and place the herbs on top of peas and put one cup of hot broth in bowl and cook dumpling and then pour olive oil in each bowl. Sprinkle bowl with grated Parmesan. Enjoy!

Baked Pasta Casserole Recipe

Ingredients

Olive oil
¾ pound wheat pasta
Sea salt
1 yellow onion
2 cloves chopped garlic,

4 cups chopped spinach
1½ cups almonds
2 lemons
8 ounces shredded mozzarella

Method

First, you have to preheat the oven and butter a large casserole dish. Then boil pasta in salt water. At this time heat olive oil and sauté the onion with salt and then put the garlic, spinach and cook for 20 minutes. Pour 1 cup almond and add pasta and mix well. Now sprinkle the bottom of pan with zest and then add layer of pasta with more cheese. Cover with a foil and bake for 30 minutes. Serve sprinkled with the remaining almonds. Enjoy!

$\mathcal{A}$ TOMATO SOUP

This sweet and tangy tomato soup is much-loved by everyone and it makes up for a whole meal by itself.

Ingredients

4 tablespoon of unsalted butter
2 medium- yellow onions
1 teaspoon sea salt
3 teaspoon -curry powder
1 teaspoon coriander

1 teaspoon cumin
½ teaspoon flakes chili
2 cans tomatoes
1 14-ounce can milk of coconut

Directions

Take pot and melt butter in it. Add the onion and salt and stir onion till it is soft and brown. Mix in the curry powder, cumin, coriander and chili flakes and cook till spices are fragrant. Then put in tomato juice and water and simmer for 15 minutes. Add coconut milk and adjust salt as per taste. This tomato soup is great if served with topped with some cream. Enjoy!

$\mathcal{B}$AKED FARRO RISOTTO RECIPE

Ingredients

2 tablespoons olive oil
One lemon
1 medium size onion
Sea salt
300 g semi-pearled farro

225 g tomato sauce
4 cups vegetable broth
½ cup grated Parmesan
1 tablespoon oregano

Directions

First preheat the oven to 205 degrees C and then rub olive oil in baking dish and sprinkle with zest of lemon. Take the large saucepan and heat the olive oil, salt and onion cook till the onion is soft. Add the faro and put the tomato puree in and broth let it simmer. Add the cheese in it and now transfer it to the prepared baking dish and bake it for 45 minutes. Serve it with cheese and oregano. Enjoy!

$\mathcal{T}$EMPEH CURRY RECIPE

Ingredients

1½ pounds waxy potatoes
2 teaspoons sea salt
8 ounces of tempeh
cilantro
1 tablespoon butter

2 tablespoons olive oil
1 yellow onion
1 teaspoon cumin seeds
1 teaspoon of curry powder
¼ teaspoon of turmeric

½ teaspoon of cayenne pepper
1 cup diced tomatoes

¾ cup of water
dollop of cream

Directions

First, you have to place the potatoes in a steamer and sprinkle with salt and cook for 20 minutes. And then take skillet and melt butter in it. Add the onion to the skillet and pour in the cumin seeds, turmeric, and curry powder for 30 seconds. Put the tomatoes, salt and water and remove from heat and add to the tempeh and let simmer for 5 minutes. Add potatoes an mix well. Serve sprinkled with cilantro. Enjoy!

SUMMER GREEN BEAN SALAD RECIPE

Ingredients

¾ green beans
1 teaspoon chopped chives
¼ teaspoon chopped thyme
1 tablespoon shallots
2 tablespoons of lemon juice
2 tablespoons of heavy cream
¼ teaspoon of salt

Pinch of ground pepper
⅓ cup of olive oil
1 teaspoon of honey
frisee
Small cherry tomatoes
½ cup of hazelnuts

Directions

Whisk thyme, chives, lemon juice, shallots, salt, pepper and heavy cream in a bowl. Whisk in the olive oil with a fork and now taste and adjust seasoning. Boil water and pour the green beans in it. Then toss green beans with the frisee and hazelnuts with splash of dressing. Toss the tomatoes in and mix well. Your dish is ready to serve. Enjoy!

CHERRY TOMATO COUSCOUS RECIPE

This recipe has sweet and tangy taste and it is loved by kids and adults alike. It is a good option for breakfast.

Ingredients

3 cups couscous
½ basket cherry tomatoes
1 cucumber
1 cup chickpeas
1 lemon

¼ cup olive oil
Sea salt
Ground pepper
⅓ cup cilantro
⅓ cup cheese

Directions

Mix the couscous, cucumber, tomatoes, and chickpeas in large mixing bowl. Squeezes lemon juice directly into mixing bowl, then add olive oil, and salt and ground pepper. Then you have to toss it well, and season accordingly. This actually needs a little amount of salt. Add basil and feta and toss gently. Serve immediately. Enjoy!

GREEN GRAM YOGA BOWL

Ingredients

Greek yogurt-1 cup
Minced ginger-½ tablespoon
Seeded serrano chile-½
Cilantro, plus more for serving-½ cup
Green onion tops-¼ cup
Spinach-½ cup
Fine grain sea salt-1 teaspoon

Cooked green gram beans-5 to 6 cups
Cooked quinoa-1 cup
Toasted almonds and/or pepitas-⅓ cup
Warmed olive oil-3 tablespoons
Smoked paprika-1½ teaspoons
Lots of freshly squeezed lime juice

Method

Combine the chili, yogurt, ginger, cilantro, green onion tops, salt, spinach, and salt in a blender. Keep blending until smooth. In a large bowl, green gram beans and quinoa are poured. Sprinkle the nuts in the bowl. Season with some salt and lime juice and mix well. Serve immediately. Enjoy!

PLUOT SUMMER SALAD

This salad is extremely hydrating and is ideal for summers.

Ingredients

Clarified butter or extra-virgin coconut oil- 2 tablespoons
Medium shallots, peeled and thinly sliced-4
Medium garlic very thinly sliced cloves -3
Chunk of peeled and nicely minced ginger-½ inch
Fresh lime juice-1½ teaspoons

Soy sauce / shoyu-2teaspoons
Runny honey-2 teaspoons
Ripe pluots, pitted and torn-5
Pitted cherries, torn in half-1 cup
Dried thinly sliced figs, stemmed -4
Toasted and chopped peanuts -½ cup
A small handful of each, chopped - fresh basil, mint, and cilantro

Method

Put the butter or oil in a large skillet, and cook the shallots, stirring regularly. Add in the garlic cloves, allow to cook for another minute or two, and then stir in the ginger for the final minute. The lime juice, soy sauce, along with honey is mixed in a small bowl. If needed, taste and adjust. Toss very gently. Then drizzle with half of the soy dressing. Serve garnished with the remaining peanuts and herbs. Enjoy!

PLUOT & POPPY YOGURT BOWL RECIPE

Ingredients

Plain Greek yogurt-10 cup
Thinly sliced pluot-1
Chopped dill-1 tablespoon
Pinch of sea salt

Toasted rolled oats-3 tablespoons
Poppy seeds-1 teaspoon
A thick drizzle of honey

Method

Stir the dill and a pinch of salt into the yogurt. Add in rest of the ingredients and mix well. Chill and serve immediately. Enjoy!

AVOCADO COCONUT OIL TARTINE RECIPE

This recipe is quickly transformed by an easy, simple twist into something completely new. It is a satiating and healthy dish for a nourishing breakfast

Ingredients

Toasted and chopped macadamia nuts-¾ cup
Small clove finely grated garlic-1
Zest of one medium orange
Squash blossoms, cut into chiffonade-4
Fine grain sea salt, or to taste-½ teaspoon

Good levain bread, sliced ¾-inch thick-4 slices
Pure virgin coconut oil-4 tablespoons
Ripe avocados, halved, pits removed-2
Slivered scallions-4

Method

The macadamia nuts, garlic, orange zest, squash blossoms and salt are combined in a small bowl and mix thoroughly. Spoon and smash half an avocado onto each piece of toast, then evenly distribute the nut mixture equally as well .Toast the bread (alternately, a broiler, or grill will work).. Finish with a sprinkling of scallions, a drizzle of olive oil . Enjoy!

CALIFORNIA BARLEY BOWL

Ingredients

Cooked barley-6 cups
Arugula or bean sprouts-4 cups
cotija, queso fresco, or ricotta salata cheese-6 ounces

Toasted almonds, or a mix of seeds/ nuts-1 cup
Fine grain sea salt, or to taste-½ teaspoon
Plain yogurt-2 cups

Zest of one lemon
Freshly squeezed lemon juice-1 tablespoon

Chives, plus more for serving-¼ cup
Fine grain sea salt-¼ teaspoon
Ripe avocados, thinly sliced-2

Method

The barley, arugula, cheese, almonds, and salt together are mixed well in a large bowl. Make a quick yogurt sauce by whisking together the yogurt, lemon zest, lemon, juice, chives, and salt in a small bowl. Serve topped with avocado, chives, and big dollops of yogurt sauce. Enjoy!

A Good Winter Salad

Ingredients

Delicate squash, seeded and sliced into thin crescents-1
Heads little gem lettuces-6 to 8
Shredded endives-2
Medium cloves of garlic-2

Fine grain sea salt-1/8 teaspoon
Melted butter-5 tablespoons
Squeeze of lemon juice-1 big
Toasted pepitas-½ cup
Ripe avocados, slivered-2

Method

Crush the garlic with the salt into a paste .Butter is melted and poured into the garlic paste. Taste and add more salt if needed. When it is ready to serve, Place the lettuce, squash, endives and pepitas in a bowl and top with the butter garlic sauce. Serve immediately. Enjoy!

Roasted Squash, Chile, and Mozzarella Salad

Ingredients

Delicate squash, scrubbed, sliced lengthwise and seeded-2 medium
Extra virgin olive oil-3 tablespoons
Smashed and peeled garlic cloves -2
Dried slivered chilies,-2 to 3

Fresh thyme sprigs, plus more for serving-2
Fine grain sea salt-¼ teaspoon
Ball of buffalo mozzarella-8 ounce
Arugula-4 cups

Method

Shred the delicate squash into ½ -inch thick crescents. Toss them in a bowl with the olive oil, garlic, chilies, thyme, and salt. Arrange in a single layer on a baking sheet. To serve, toss the arugula with the squash with a splash of olive oil. Toss until nicely coated, then tear the mozzarella ball apart, and gently toss it with the squash as well. Season with more salt, and serve topped with some slivered scallions. Enjoy!

*I*MMUNITY SOUP

The name of this recipe is justified by the nutrition content in it. This is an excellent health soup for kids, especially during winter.

Ingredients

Extra virgin olive oil-1 tablespoon
Medium onion, quartered and thinly sliced-1
Thinly sliced stalks-3 celery
Carrot, thinly sliced-1
Medium garlic sliced cloves-8

Grated peeled ginger,-2 tablespoons
Finely ground white pepper, plus more to taste-¾ teaspoon
Trimmed mushrooms-1½ cups
Firm tofu, sliced into thin slabs-8 ounces
Fine grain sea salt-2½ teaspoons

Method

Heat the oil in a large soup pot over medium heat, and stir in the onion, celery, carrot, garlic, and ginger. Gently sauté just until soft, Add a small splash of water. Add some white pepper and 10 cups of water, constantly stirring. Simmer for about 15 minutes. Add the mushrooms, tofu, and salt, and gently cook for another 5 minutes. Stir well, taste, and adjust seasoning and consistency. Ladle the soup into shallow soup bowls and top with lots of the solid ingredients. Add a drizzle of olive oil just before serving. Enjoy!

*M*ISO TAHINI SOUP

Ingredients

Water-4 cups
White miso, or to taste-4 tablespoons
tahini- ¼ cup
Small-medium delicate squash, seeded and sliced into ¼-inch crescents-1
Medium white turnip, peeled and cut into ¾-inch pieces-1

Zest of one lemon
Cooked brown rice-3 cups
Sliced avocado-1
Bunch of minced chives, -1
Toasted nori (or kale), crumbled, for serving
Toasted sesame seeds

Method

Add the squash and turnips to a large pot, cover with the water and boil until the vegetables are tender. Reduce the heat and simmer for about 15 minutes. Remove the pot from the heat and let it cool just slightly. Add a few tablespoons of the hot water in a small bowl and add the miso and whisk. Stir the thinned miso back into the pot along with the Tahiti, and lemon zest. At this point, taste, and adjust the broth to your liking. Ladle the broth over the vegetables, and finish with a few slices of avocado, a sprinkling of chives, toasted nori, and sesame seeds. Place a generous scoop of rice with some of the squash and turnips and serve. Enjoy!

PERSIAN YOGURT SOUP

Ingredients

1 Small onion or 6 peeled shallots, grated on box grater
Full fat plain yogurt, room temperature-4 cups
Brown rice, well rinsed-½ cup
Yellow split peas, well rinsed-½ cup
Flour or organic cornstarch-1 tablespoon
Barely warm water-4½ cups
Fine grain sea salt-1½ teaspoons
Freshly ground pepper-½ teaspoons

Chopped green onions-¾ cup
Parsley or cilantro-½ cup
Chopped dill or fennel fronds-¼ cup
Cooked chickpeas, or more to your liking- 2cups
Unsalted butter-4 tablespoons
Medium cloves garlic, finely chopped- 3
Dried mint-1 tablespoon
Generous pinch of salt
Toasted sesame seeds

Method

Use your thickest-bottomed soup pot or casserole here. Thin pans will make this tricky. To the cold pan add the shallots, yogurt, rice, split peas, and flour. Stir in the water and cook over low-medium heat. It should thicken a bit at this point. Stir until well combined and uniform. Keep heating it on low heat, barely any bubbling, stirring, stirring until the rice is cooked through. Ladle into a bowl and serve hot. Enjoy!

SUMMER VEGETABLE CURRY

Ingredients

Can coconut milk-1(14 ounce)
Medium shallots, chopped-4
Green curry paste, or more to taste-2 tablespoons
Sea salt-½ teaspoon
Waxy potatoes, washed and sliced ½ -inch thick-½ pound
Yellow (or green) beans-¼ pound

Romanesco florets (or broccoli)-¼ pound
Extra firm tofu, cut into ¼ inch cubes-8 ounces
Kernels from 1 ear of corn
Quartered lime-1
Fresh coriander seeds (or chopped cilantro)

Method

Spoon a few tablespoons of thick coconut cream from the top of the coconut milk, place it in a large pot over medium-high heat and bring to a simmer. Stir in the curry paste and salt, and cook for another minute or two. Add 2/3 of the shallots and sauté until they soften a bit, for 2-3 minutes - adding more curry paste or salt if needed. Add the rest of the coconut milk to the pot along with the potatoes, and cover .Squeeze some lime juice over remaining shallots and set aside. Serve with a side of the lemon-y shallots. Enjoy!

GINGER COCONUT MILK SOUP RECIPE

The ginger-spiked coconut broth is an easy-going companion with rice, noodles, rice, vegetables, and grains.

Ingredients

Dried pasta noodles -2 ounce
Cans full-fat coconut milk-2 (14 ounce)
Patty pan squashes, cut into small cubes-2
Broccoli florets-20
Asparagus tips-16
Sliced scallions -3

Can water (use the coconut can to measure)-1(14 ounce)
Knob of ginger, peeled and grated -2 inch
Minced shallots-3 large
Fine grain sea salt, or to taste-1½ teaspoons

Method

Salt well, and cook the pasta per package instructions. Bring a big pot of water to a boil. Drain and set aside. Bring the coconut milk, water, ginger, shallots, and salt to a gentle boil. Heat and simmer for five to ten minutes. Add the vegetables to the simmering coconut milk, Just a couple of minutes before you're ready to serve and cook until just tender, a minute or so. Arrange a pile of noodles in each bowl, and ladle vegetables and broth on top. Finish with a generous squeeze of lime and lots of cilantro. Enjoy!

BLACK PEPPER CAULIFLOWER SALAD

Ingredients

Red wine vinegar-¼ cup
Extra-virgin olive oil -⅓ cup
Fine grain sea salt -¾ teaspoon
Black crushed peppercorns-1 tablespoon
Head of cauliflower, cut into tiny florets-2 pounds

Diced red onion-¾ cup
Toasted pistachios, roughly chopped -1 cup
Crumbled feta cheese-½ cup
Diced apples-3
Black olives-⅓ cup

Method

Bring a pot of water to a boil, salt well and cook the cauliflower for a minute. Place under cold water after it is drained, and set aside. The red onion olive oil, salt, and black pepper are mixed in a sauce pan. Once the onions have turned pink and infused the oil and vinegar mixture, remove from heat and set aside. The pistachios, feta, apples, olives, and 2/3 of the red onion vinaigrette are mixed. Toss everything together gently and serve immediately. Enjoy!

Olive Oil Braised Spring Vegetables

Ingredients

Extra virgin olive oil-2 cups
Baby potatoes, cut into bite-friendly segments-¼ pound
Quartered, trimmed baby fennel-2
Fine grain sea salt-¼ teaspoon
Baby carrots, cut into bite-friendly segments-¼ pound

Small spring trimmed onions (or scallions), -6
Asparagus, trimmed and cut into segments-½ pound
Lemon, cut into small wedges, deseeded-1

Method

The olive oil is heated in a large skillet over medium-low heat. Add your long-cooking vegetables to the pan. Add the onions, then cover and cook for another 10 - 15 minutes. Add the asparagus and a few of the lemon wedges to the pan. Add the carrots and potatoes cook just until it brightens, and is barely tender. Remove from heat and sprinkle with herbs (dill or thyme). Serve with the remaining lemon wedges on the side. Enjoy!

Miso Oat Porridge

Ingredients

Unsalted butter-1 tablespoon
Rolled oats-1½ cups
Water-3 cups
miso, or to taste-1 tablespoons

Toppings: lots of toasted walnuts, minced chives, shaved radishes, cream or crème fraiche

Method

Heat the butter in a medium saucepan, stirring in the oats, and patiently cook until the oats get fragrant and well-toasted. Simmer until absorbed. Place the miso in a separate bowl, and scoop a few big spoonfuls of the oats. Remove from heat. Stir well, and thoroughly fold this miso back into main pot of oats. Adjust the seasoning. Serve topped with minced chives, radishes, walnuts, and a good drizzle of cream. Enjoy!

Thinnest Oatmeal Cookies

Ingredients

Whole wheat flour-2 tablespoons
Baking powder-1 teaspoon
Fine grain sea salt-¼ teaspoon
Fennel crushed seeds-1 teaspoon

Poppy seeds-4 teaspoons
Unsalted butter-½ cup
Uncooked rolled oats (not instant)-1½ cup
Natural cane sugar-2/3 cup

Method

In a medium saucepan gently melt the butter, combine the flour in a small bowl. In a large bowl, whisk the sugar into the flour mixture, and then add the oats. Stir until combined and add in rest of the ingredients and mix well. Scoop out 1 tablespoon of the dough at a time drop onto the prepared baking sheets, at least 2 inches apart. Bake until very deeply golden, about 8-10 minutes. Remove, and cool to room temperature and serve. Enjoy!

Toasted Almond Sables

Ingredients

Salted softened butter, - 2 sticks
Sugar - 100 g
Fine sea salt - ¼ teaspoon
Pure extract vanilla –1 teaspoon

Currants-½ cup
Large grain sugar, for sprinkling
Unbleached all-purpose flour - 130 g
Whole wheat flour - scant 1 cup

How to make?

In a medium bowl, whisk together the all-purpose and whole wheat flours. Set aside. Beat the butter with the sugar, salt and vanilla, until smooth and creamy. Stir in the almonds. Add the flour and mix until barely combined. Add the currants and stir. Stamp into desired shapes. Place cookies at least an inch apart on prepared baking sheets, sprinkle each cookie with a pinch of large-grain sugar, and chill them in the freezer one last time for another ten minutes. Enjoy!

Biscotti al Pistachio

Ingredients

Raw pistachios - 500g
Granulated sugar - 200g
Vanilla extract -1 teaspoon
Freshly grated lemon zest - 1½ teaspoon

Confectioners' sugar, for coating cookies-
1 cup
Honey -1 tablespoon

Method

Pulse the pistachios in a food processor until the nuts are finely chopped. Combine the ground pistachio-sugar mixture with the honey, vanilla, and lemon zest in a large mixing bowl until the dough is well combined and soft. At this point, add the rest of the granulated sugar and mix gently.

Form the dough into small balls, and roll them in the confectioners' sugar to coat well. Transfer the balls to cookies sheets lined with parchment paper, leaving at least an inch between each cookie. Bake for 15-18 minutes. In a sealed container these cookies can be stored for up to 2 weeks. Enjoy!

Olive Biscuit Cookies

Ingredients

Powdered, sifted sugar – 1 cup
Extra-virgin olive oil - 1 tablespoon
Unsalted butter, room temperature -9 tablespoons

All-purpose flour – 1 cup
Cured pitted and chopped olives – 5
Two pinches of sea salt

Method

Combine the sugar and olive oil and whisk until combined. Use a wooden spoon to stir in the flour by hand, just until the dough is smooth. The olives and salt are added. Keep stirring .Place the dough in the middle of a large piece of parchment paper. Bake until the edges of the cookies are golden, rotating the pans from top to bottom, front to back once after about 8 minutes. Remove from the oven and cool before removing from the baking sheet. Makes a few dozen tiny cookies. Enjoy!

Broccoli-Basil Mac and Cheese

Ingredients

Butternut, or other winter squash, peeled, seeded and acorn, cut into tiny chunks-1 small
Olive oil
Basil-1 bunch
Good brown bread-2 slices

Head of broccoli (100 g / 3.5 oz.), roughly chopped-½ small
Crème fraiche or sour cream-4 tablespoons
Grated white cheddar cheese-100g
Grated gruyere cheese-100g
Large handful of (yellow) cherry tomatoes
(Whole wheat) macaroni elbows-300g

Method

Place the squash on a large baking sheet, and then drizzle with a bit of olive oil, salt and pepper, and bake until golden. In the meantime, pulse half the basil, all of the bread, the broccoli and a lug of olive oil in a food processor. In a separate bowl, the crème fraiche and grated cheeses are combined. Boil the pasta in well-salted water for a bit less time. Place the cherry tomatoes in the food processor with the remaining basil .Pulse a couple times to break things up, then add to the crème fraise mixture and stir well. The cheese mixture is added to the hot pasta. Add the squash and give it a good stir. Serve hot. Enjoy!

Pomegranate Yogurt Bowl

Pomegranate and Yogurt are good combination for a good heath as well as soothe your taste buds.

Ingredients

Greek yogurt- 1 big dollop

fresh pomegranate juice -2 tablespoons

honey - a drizzle
puffed quinoa crisps - a handful
toasted sunflower seeds

pomegranate seeds, whole
rose petals, fresh or dried
bee pollen, a bit

Method

First, take a shallow bowl. Pour Greek yogurt and swirl pomegranate juice along with honey in the yogurt. Then the cereal has to be sprinkled on it. Add a bit of sunflower seeds. At the end, add some rose petals, either dried or fresh and also the bee pollen. Taste the dish a bit and add the cereals, bee pollen and rose petals some more, if it is required for more taste. Serve chilled. Enjoy!

DETOXIFYING MINT TEA

Ingredients

Dry mixture

coriander seeds- 4 teaspoons
fennel seeds- 4 teaspoons
whole cumin seeds- 1½ teaspoons
black peppercorns- 2 teaspoons

Fresh ingredients

ginger slices 3
fresh mint leaves- 16
Lemon -3 thin slices

Method

Blend the dry mixture ingredients i.e. fennel seeds, coriander seeds, cumin seeds and black peppercorns in a jar. Mix them well and set aside in an air tight jar.

Boil 2 cups of water. Mix ginger with mint and break them a little using mortar pestle. Add the dry mixture ingredients and the ginger-mint mixture. Boil for 3-5 minutes. Cover the pot and remove from heat. Put lemon slices in a strainer. After that, strain tea through lemon in a container. Enjoy!

GIN-MARINATED OLIVES

Ingredients

12 ounces - green olives, drained, rinsed
Serrano peppers- 2
1 garlic clove, sliced thinly
1 lemon- slivered peel
6 tablespoons olive oil extra virgin

Gin- ½ cup
Oregano- ½ teaspoon dried
dried thyme- a few sprigs
cubed feta cheese- ¼ cup

Method

Heat the oven to 180 C. In baking dish, place olives in single layer. Mix them with garlic, peppers, lemon peel, gin, olive oil, oregano and thyme. Toss the mixture well. Then bake for nearly 30 min, cautiously jostling for a single time or maybe twice. Remove from the oven. Then sprinkle with feta cubes. Let it reach room temperature or cool it before serving. Enjoy!

GIANT LEMON FENNEL BEANS

Ingredients

4-5 fennel bulbs (small)
2 teaspoons virgin olive oil
¼ teaspoon fine salt
1 teaspoon honey
Half sliced lemon

Dry white wine- ¼ cup
cooked white beans- 2 cups
½ cup water from the cooking beans
½ cup chopped dill

Method

After removing the bulbs outer layer, the base of the bulb is trimmed. The olive oil is heated and then it is removed from heat and the fennel is added to it. The wedge is placed on the pan and it is cooked for two minutes until it becomes brown. It is cooked for further two minutes. After that the honey, wine, sea salt and lemon are added. It is again cooked to heat the beans. These beans are best at any temperature. Enjoy!

MISO TAHINI SOUP

Ingredients

1 small/average delicate squash, sliced into
¼-inch falcate
1 white turnip, cut into ¾-inch parts
water-4 cups
4 teaspoons white miso

tahini-¼ cup
1 lemon
Cooked rice- 3 cups
1 sliced avocado
A bunch of chives toasted nori crumbled fried sesame seeds

Cooking method

In a large pot the squash and turnips are kept and then covered with water and allowed to boil for 15 minutes. They are then removed and some hot water is poured into a bowl. The thin miso is cooked with Tahini and lemon flavor. Some extra miso will increase the saltiness.
To serve, a scoop of rice is placed in a bowl besides the squash and white turnips. At last, sprinkle some pieces of avocado, chives, toasted nori, and seeds of sesame on it. Enjoy!

AVOCADO SPRING ROLLS

Ingredients

Extra virgin olive oil- ½ cup
Oregano- ¼ cup
Parsley-¼ cup
One garlic clove
¼ teaspoon sea salt

¼ cup toasted chopped hazelnuts
cooked rice- 1 cup
6 ounces fried tofu
1 ripe avocado sliced
Rice paper wrappers- 6/8

Method of cooking

The oregano paste is made by mixing the olive oil, oregano, garlic, salt and parsley. It is cooked until it becomes smooth. The hazelnuts and cooked are rice are mixed together. The spring rolls are gathered. In bowl of hot water bowl, rice paper wrappers are dipped for 3 seconds. It is allowed to soak. It is place on a flat surface, and in the bottom of a wrapper some rice the oregano paste, some tofu strips, and avocados are arranged. Arrange on a platter and serve with some horse radish sauce. Enjoy!

LEMON CUCUMBER TOFU SALAD RECIPE

Ingredients

Lemon cucumbers- 2 sliced into ¼ inch
some fresh dill
virgin olive oil- ¼ cup
¼ cup lemon juice

Salt
8 ounces nigari firm tofu
pine nuts- ¼ cup
ripe avocado- half

Method

At first, cucumbers, lemon juice, dill, salt and olive oil are tossed. After that, the tofu is cooked in a skillet and some salt is added to it. It is heated until the pieces are browned. Combine the tofu with the lemon cucumber mix and toss well. Taste and season accordingly. Enjoy!

AVOCADO ASPARAGUS TARTINE

Ingredients

4 toasted pieces of grain bread, having olive oil and garlic
½ teaspoon- olive oil
½ lb.- asparagus stalks
One clove garlic, finely sliced

caraway seeds- ½ teaspoon
1 avocado, smashed
some arugula, cooked with olive oil
Some toasted almonds, or seeds of sunflower

Method

Some minutes before you have to eat, warm up the olive oil in a skillet over low/medium heat. When the oil heats up, put in the asparagus and a bit of salt and cook for thirty seconds. Put in the garlic along with caraway, and cook for again thirty seconds until the spears become green. Take away from heat and gather the tartines. Place a mashed avocado on every slice of bread. Keep that on the top that with a small amount of arugula, a small number of asparagus spears, and pepitas or almond seeds. Enjoy!

SPROUT SALAD

Ingredients

4 cups simple Greek yogurt
¼ teaspoon salt or more to taste
Chopped arugula
some minced chives
Green gram bean sprouts- 8 oz. about 2 cups

Some well-toasted, pieced almonds
ripe avocado-1, chopped
olive oil- extra virgin
Chive flowers (optional)

Method

In a bowl mix the yogurt, sea salt, arugula, and minced chives. In a big bowl cook the green gram beans along with almonds and olive oil and a bit of salt. Put in the avocado, and softly toss one or two times. Dish up the green gram beans beside the yogurt mixture and sprinkle with a little extra olive oil. If you buy a small number of chive flowers of a bunch, then sprinkle them over the top. Enjoy!

KALE MARKET SALAD

Ingredients

2 stalks green garlic (2 stalks) washed and sliced
¼ teaspoon or more sea salt
2 teaspoons clean lemon sap
⅓ cup virgin olive oil
2 teaspoons full-grown avocado
1 teaspoon of honey, or to flavor

Pepper to flavor
½ cluster kale, cut into pieces
1 cup cooked wheat berries
4-5 carrots, very delicately sliced
1 little corm of fennel, sliced
1 avocado, slashed into small chops
some almond slices, cooked

Method

Make the salad dressing using a hand mixer or food processor to crush the green garlic, sea salt, lemon sap, olive oil, honey along with pepper and avocado until they are soft. Taste, and season with salt, or honey, or juice of lemon

Before you are prepared to serve, mix the kale with some of the dressing in a big bowl; mix it well using your hands to soften the kale slightly in the process. Put in the carrots along with fennel, extra dressing, and some pinches of sea salt, and cook again. Taste and add some more seasoning accordingly. Enjoy!

THE GREENEST SALAD

Ingredients

1 medium head or romaine lettuce (not ripe)

1 average size of broccoli cut into little florets
One small sized avocado (pieced)
Toasted pistachios- ⅓ cup

a slight amount of crushed feta
big splatter of creamy tarragon vinaigrette

Method

Take a big pan of water to simmer; add salt as per requirement, put in the broccoli and boil for only a minute or so that the broccoli becomes bright and also soft. Keep it under cold water to stop the cooking and then dry with a cloth and keep aside.

Cut the bottom off the romaine, after that cut it diagonally into ½ inch narrow pieces of lettuce. Rinse well and dry out gently, but fully. Chill in the refrigerator, until it is ready to be eaten.

Before serving, mix the broccoli, leaves of lettuce with vinaigrette. Enjoy!

POSOLE IN BROTH

Ingredients

dried posole- ½ cups
White or golden onion- 1 medium
5 cups good tasted soup
1 Serrano chili, minced

2 cups or 12 ounces of toasted mung beans, not obligatory
1 cluster of scallions, pieced and sliced

Method

To heat the posole kernels, wash and choose the kernels, cover up with water and then allow soaking for about `six hours, or for a night. Put in a big pot along with the onion, cut in two and strip, and cover with a little amount of water. Boil it and roast for nearly one hour, so that a good amount of the kernels bloom. The broth and the onion should be kept aside. If you are cooking it before time, the broth as well as the toasted posole kernels freezes well.

To serve, garnish with chopped up olives, wedged avocado, shoots or micro greens, cooked wedged almonds, and sprinkle of olive oil or lemon oil. Enjoy!

AN IDEAL LUNCH SALAD

Ingredients

Celery stalks-3, very delicately sliced
Chickpeas- 1 cup drained or washed
arugula or sliced romaine lettuce- 3 handfuls
⅓ cup toasted pepitas/almonds- ⅓ cup
15 black olives, sliced
Red onion, thinly diced- ½ small
1 pieces of broccoli florets, bleached

2 garlic cloves
4 tablespoons miso
2 tablespoons mirin
2 tablespoons vinegar
1 teaspoon cumin
¼ cup yoghurt
¼ cup cream

Method

In a huge bowl mix together the celery, arugula, chickpeas, olives, onion, in addition to broccoli. Put it to one side. Prepare the dressing by crushing the garlic into a coarse mixture in a mortar and grinder (or with a knife). Blend in the miso, then put in the mirin, and also vinegar, and mix until it is brought together. Put in the cumin in addition to the yogurt, and blend again prior to finish it with the fatty cream. Taste, and alter the dressing if required.

Before serving, put in some of the dressing on the ingredients we prepped before and cook well. Go on adding extra dressing according to your liking, putting the avocado at the end, therefore it upholds its structure. Enjoy!

YELLOW WAX BEANS & SCALLIONS

Ingredients

¾ pound of golden wax beans
2 teaspoons butter
¼ cup or 35 g wedged almonds
¼ cup or of 35 g pepitas

fine granule sea salt
Some small scallions (or crumbled scallions) sprinkling of fresh herbs
½ full-grown avocado, finely sliced

Method

Cut the ends from the beans, and cut into 1-inch pieces.

Warm up the butter in a big pot over medium/high heat. Mix in the almonds along with pepitas together with a bit of salt. Cook it, tossing often, to make it golden. Put in the beans, cook to coat, cover and heat for some minutes to make the beans tender enough. Shift to a serving dish or plate, serve with small scallions on the side. Enjoy!

AVOCADO COCONUT OIL TARTINE

Ingredients

¾ cup cooked and sliced macadamia nuts
1 small sized clove garlic, thinly pieced
Flavor of orange- one medium
blossoms- 4 squash slash into chiffonade
½ teaspoon well grain salt to add flavor
4 pieces good quality levain bread, pieced
¾-inch

4 teaspoons clean coconut oil
2 full-grown avocados, halved, pits removed
4 slivered scallions
olive oil, to sprinkle

Method

Mix the macadamia nuts with garlic, flavor of orange, squash blooms and salt in a bowl and blend carefully. Fry the bread (or a broil) till it becomes golden. Before serving, ensure that the bread is warm. Keep 1 teaspoon of the coconut oil on every slice and place uniformly, saturating the bread. Serve and break some part of an avocado onto every part of toast, after that consistently allocate the nut blend equally as well. At last, sprinkle the scallions, a few drops of olive oil, and get flavor you like. Enjoy!

Tofu Amaranth Salad

Ingredients

Peeled clove of garlic- ½ small
¼ teaspoon- red chili chips
¼ teaspoon fine particle sea salt, or more to add taste
1 teaspoon of sunflower oil
Scallions - 4 finely sliced
⅔ cup of fatty coconut milk
2 teaspoons of lemon juice

2-3 pieces of small lettuces, cut into ½ -inch strips
some amaranth leaves, or scarlet lettuce
some bits of more firm tofu which are dried and cut into pieces
some basil leaves
avocado, finely wedged- 1 small

Method

Begin by preparing the dressing. In a mortar and grinder crush the garlic along with chili flakes into a mixture together with the salt. Besides these, you can utilize a food processor. Pour the oil as well as the scallions, and crush or cut a little more. Remove the blend to a jar, and mix in the coconut milk and the lemon juice. Taste, and regulate with additional salt or even lemon juice if want. You can preserve the dressing in a fridge for almost seven days.

Be certain your lettuce and also amaranth is washed and the dried, then mix in a bowl together with the tofu and herb. Pour the dressing and serve immediately. Enjoy!

Avocado Salad Recipe

Ingredients

2 teaspoons oregano
2 teaspoons sea salt
5 teaspoons extra virgin olive oil
1 teaspoon freshly pressed lemon juice

2 cups toasted lentils
1-2 mature avocados, quarter piece
¼ cup toasted hazelnuts
¼ cup chives- minced

Method

Crush the oregano along with salt into a mixture in a crusher. Slowly cook in the olive oil and after that add the lemon juice. Cook the lentils with 2 teaspoons of the oregano oil. Place on a dish or in a bowl. Now before serving, slash the avocado into the quarter piece, then cut quite finely, and keep on surface of the lentils. Sprinkle with some drops of the oil, after that drop over the hazelnuts, in addition to chives. A final sprinkle of oil may be required. Enjoy!

MOROCCAN CHICKPEA SOUP

This recipe is a complete vegan recipe that tastes totally different and is packed with many essential nutrients.

Ingredients

2 tablespoons Olive oil
A medium sized onion, chopped
2 sticks of celery
1 teaspoon Cumin, ground
2 cups Vegetable stock

1 can of chopped plum tomatoes with garlic
1 can of chickpeas
Broad beans, frozen
Lemon zest and juice
Parsley

Method

The oil is to be heated in the saucepan and fry the chopped onions in it with celery for about 10 minutes. When they are softened, add the cumin and cook for a minute. Then the stock, tomatoes and the chickpeas are to be added to the pan and sprinkle the pepper over it. Season to taste and then add the lemon zest with the other herbs. This healthy soup is can be an ideal choice to be served with a flatbread. Enjoy!

MINESTRONE SOUP

This easy to cook recipe is a main meal soup that is also a vegan recipe and is very delicious. Moreover this meat-free soup gives loads of essential nutrients.

Ingredients

1 can Vegetable stock
1 tin of chopped tomatoes
1 packet Spaghetti, cut lengthwise
A drizzle Olive oil
Parmesan-style cheese, grated, for garnish

2 cups Mixed vegetables, frozen
4 tbsp. Pesto

Method

Pour the vegetable stock in a pot and bring it to boil with the spaghetti and the tomatoes. Before the pasta is ready, add the vegetables and again boil them and cook them until properly cooked. When cooked, serve it in the bowl and sprinkle the pesto, olive oil and the grated parmesan-style cheese over it. This delicious and healthy soup is ready to serve. Enjoy!

SPICY ROOT AND LENTIL CASSEROLE

This easy to cook recipe is packed with a great nutritional value in it and the ingredients used are easily available.

Ingredients

2 tablespoons Vegetable oil
An onion, chopped
2 cloves of garlic, minced
3-4 Potatoes, peeled and cut in cubes
3-4 carrots, diced
2 parsnips, sliced

2 teaspoons Curry paste/powder
2 cups Vegetable stock
1 cup Red lentils,
1 teaspoon Coriander, chopped
Low fat yogurt and flat bread to serve

Method

The oil is to be heated in the pan and the onions and garlic are to be cooked in it. When they are softened, add the potatoes, carrots and parsnips to it and cook for about 7-8 minutes. When the vegetables are golden in color, add the curry paste to it and add the vegetable stock to it and then bring it to boil. When boiled, add the lentils and cook by covering the pan for 20 minutes on a low heat. When the sauce is thickened, stir the coriander into it and season to taste and then heat it thoroughly. When cooked add the yogurt and some coriander and serve it with flat bread. Enjoy!

SPICED POTATOES WITH CABBAGE AND COCONUT

Ingredients

4 Potatoes, halved and unpeeled
Sunflower oil, for frying
1 pinch Asafetida
1 teaspoon Mustard seeds
1 teaspoon Cumin seeds

4-5 Dried red chilies
A head cabbage
Coconut, freshly shaved and toasted, for garnish
Coriander, for garnish

Method

The potatoes are to be cooked in a pot of salted water for about 10 minutes. When the potatoes are softened, drain the water from the potatoes and place them in a pan and crush them lightly. Then heat oil, add asafetida to it with spices and dried chilies. Cook for few minutes. When the chilies darken, add the fresh chili, cabbage and salt and cook again for few minutes. Then the potatoes are to be added. When cooked, add the lemon juice, coconut and coriander to it and serve. Enjoy!

CORNMEAL BREADED ZUCCHINI FRIES

This tasty, healthy, meat free snack and is very easy to be prepare and all the ingredients used are also easily found.

Ingredients

1 medium sized zucchini
1 cup of cornmeal
½ teaspoon chili powder
½ teaspoon garlic salt

Water, as required

Method

The oven is to be preheated to 350 degrees F and the cookie sheet is to be kept greased. Take a small bowl and mix the cornmeal, chili powder, garlic salt in it properly and set it at a side. Then thickly slice the zucchinis to sticks and dip each of the sticks in water. Then take each slice of zucchini and coat it in the cornmeal mixture. When coated, place them in the cookie sheet and bake them in the oven until golden-brown in color. Serve when the zucchini fries are ready. Enjoy!

PUMPKIN LATTE

This beverage is purely vegetarian recipe which is very delicious to taste and at the same time is very healthy. And you do not need to have it only when Halloween rolls around!

Ingredients

1 tablespoon of pureed pumpkin
½ teaspoon of cinnamon
½ cup of soymilk
A pinch nutmeg

Sugar
1 cup of fresh coffee
Vegan cream, whipped

Method

Take a bowl and add the pumpkin, soymilk, cinnamon, sugar and nutmeg to it and mix them. Warm it until steamy, then add this mixture to the cup of coffee and top it with whipped cream and cinnamon. The pumpkin latte is ready to be served. Enjoy!

DANK CURRY COCOA MIX

This delicious to taste beverage is easy to be prepare and is also very healthy.

Ingredients

About two cup of organic dark brown sugar
1 cup of cocoa, unsweetened

Sea salt
Curry powder

Method

Take all the ingredients in a small sized bowl and mix them properly, until all the ingredients are combined well with each other. This can also be done using a blender, and have to ensure that no lumps should remain in the mixture. Then store the dry mixture in a container. When serving, add few spoons of the mixture to the glass and add the soymilk over it. To add few more flavors, sprinkle some cinnamon sugar over it when serving. Enjoy!

GREEN GODDESS SMOOTHIE

This green smoothie is rich in nutrients and is also very delicious to taste. This smoothie can also be served to your friends and family as welcome drinks, and this green smoothie will definitely be liked by them.

Ingredients

1 ripe banana
1 cup of spinach
½ cup of red, green, yellow bell peppers
1 Cucumber, chopped

1 Orange, chopped
½ cup of non-diary milk
Water, as required

Method

Take a blender and put the banana, spinach, bell pepper, cucumber, orange, milk and required water to it and blend in a low speed and gradually increase the speed, until all the ingredients are mixed thoroughly. When the creamy texture of the smoothie is formed, serve it in your favorite smoothie glass. Enjoy!

CHEESY PESTO PIZZA

Ingredients

Fresh leaves of basil
1 cup of pine nuts
2 medium cloves of garlic
Olive oil
Salt

A French baguette
1 cup of tomato sauce
1 cup of vegan mozzarella cheese, shredded

Method

Process the basil leaves with garlic and pine nuts in a food processor. When they are chopped, add the olive oil and salt and process it again for about 10 minutes. The oven is to be preheated and the baking dish is to be kept ready. Then the baguette is to be sliced and then place them to the baking dish and then make another layer over the baguette with the pesto, then top the pesto with sauce and then spread the chees over them and broil it for about 7-8 minutes. When the cheese is melted, allow to cool and serve. Enjoy!

WHOLE WHEAT PIZZA CRUST

This pizza crust is not only delicious to taste but is very healthy and moreover this meat free pizza can be enjoyed by everyone.

Ingredients

About 2 teaspoons of active dry yeast

1 cup of warm water

2 cup of whole wheat flour
1 teaspoon Wheat germ
2 tablespoons Brown rice syrup

1 Garlic clove
1 tablespoon Olive oil

Method

The yeast is to be dissolved in warm water in a small bowl. When creamy, set it aside for about 10-15 minutes. In the meantime, mix together the flour, wheat germ and salt. When completely mixed, add the dissolved yeast to it with the brown rice syrup. Then, grate the garlic and add it to the mixture and also add the olive oil to it and set it aside to rise. Keep it at least for an hour, then then roll the dough and place it in the baking dish. Bake it and when baked, add your favorite topping over it before serving. Enjoy!

MANGO CUSTARD

Ingredients

1 can of coconut milk
Agave syrup, 2-3 tbsp.
2-3 mangoes, peeled and sliced

½ cup of ice
Agar-agar powder, 2 teaspoon

Method

Take a pot and bring the coconut milk and the agave syrup to boil. In the meantime the mango and the ice cubes are to be blended in the blender. Then, reduce the heat of the coconut milk and add the agar-agar powder to the mixture. When they are dissolved, combine both the mixture of coconut milk and mango in a blender and blend well. When blended completely, transfer it to bowls and refrigerate them at least for an hour. Then serve chilled. Enjoy!

SPICED GRILLED CAULIFLOWER STEAK

This delicious dish is crispy, crunchy and makes for a delicious appetizer.

Ingredients

A large sized cauliflower
1 tablespoon of cumin
1 tablespoon of coriander
1 teaspoon of red pepper flakes

A clove of garlic, minced
Salt and pepper, to taste
1 tablespoon of olive oil or any oil
proffered by you

Method

The cauliflower is to be sliced lengthwise in steaks. Then mix the dry herbs in a small bowl and rub it over the steaks. Then sprinkle the oil and rub the minced garlic over it. Keep the coated cauliflower aside for few minutes. Now, the coated cauliflower is to be grilled for about 5-10 minutes. Serve it hot. Enjoy!

GRILLED ASPARAGUS

This vegetarian recipe is very delicious and healthy. Moreover all the ingredients needed to make this dish are easily available.

Ingredients

A pound of fresh trimmed asparagus   Salt
Olive oil   Pepper

Method

The grill is to be pre-heated. Now, take a dinner plate, and place the asparagus on the plate. Sprinkle the olive oil over it and sprinkle some salt and pepper over it. With the help of your hands, mix them properly with the asparagus. Then keep it at a side, until the grill is heated. Then transfer the asparagus directly to the grill plate. When grilled take them out and serve it. For more fried and crisp effect the grill time can be extended. Enjoy!

COCONUT MANGO RICE

This unique flavor of rice is very delicious to taste and will definitely be loved by everyone.

Ingredients

About 2 cups of coconut milk   1 teaspoon of nutmeg, grated
1 cup of basmati or any other long   A chopped ripe mango
grained rice, uncooked

Method

Take a pot and slowly boil the coconut milk, then the rice and the grated nutmeg is to be added to the pot, again bring them to boil. When bubbling, lower the heat and cook it by covering the pot for about 20 minutes. When the rice is cooked, take the pot away from the heat and add the chopped mangoes and then stir it properly with the cooked rice. Before serving the coconut mango rice, let it cool for at least 5-10 minutes. Enjoy!

BAKED SPINACH RISOTTO

This recipe us amazingly delicious and is easy to cook. The ingredients are also readily available.

Ingredients

2 cups of cooked rice   2 cloves of garlic, minced
A packet of frozen spinach   1 teaspoon of cayenne pepper
½ pound of tofu
Olive oil
Onion, chopped

Method

The oven is to be preheated to 325 degrees F. Now take a blender and add the tofu, olive oil and spinach to it and blend them well, until a creamy texture is formed. Now, take a pan and heat the oil in it and sauté the chopped onions and garlic in it. Now take the rice, pepper and spices with spinach together and stir them with the creamy tofu. When the rice is mixed with the mixture, transfer it to a baking dish that was already greased with cooking spray. Then place the baking dish in the preheated oven and bake it for about 30 minutes. When cooked, the delicious to taste vegan recipe of risotto is ready to serve. Enjoy!

AVOCADO CUCUMBER MAKI AND SWEET POTATO NIGIRI

This delicious appetizer is a super hit at parties. Who said sushi cannot be vegetarian?

Ingredients

About 2 cups of cooked brown rice
Juice of a lemon
About 2 teaspoon of agave
23 sheets of nori

A cucumber, sliced
Sesame seeds, toasted
A sweet potato, boiled, peeled and cut in cubes

Method

Take the cooked rice and add the lemon juice in it and stir it properly, then add the agave and mix it again. After mixing them in the rice, set aside and let the rice cool for about an hour. To prepare the right side of the maki, take a bamboo mat and place the sheet of nori over it and then take a handful of rice and place it at the center of the sheet. Then line the rice, cucumber over it with the avocado and then roll the nori sheet upwards. Chill it in the refrigerator. For the preparation of the nigiri, the sweet potatoes are to be chilled and then mold the rice in shape of prism and chill it. When both the maki and nigiri is ready, serve it. Enjoy!

SIMPLE STUFFED MUSHROOMS

This delicious to taste, meat free appetizers are easy to cook and the ingredients are readily available. This recipe will be enjoyed by people of all age groups.

Ingredients

1 can of 3 pounds of mushroom
An onion
2 cloves of garlic
Parsley

Vegetable oil
Breadcrumbs
Salt and pepper, to taste

Method

The mushrooms are to be cleansed and the stems are to be removed. The oven is to be preheated to 400 F and the cookie sheet is also to be greased with oil. The cleaned mushrooms are to be placed on the greased cookie sheet. Now, take a food processor and chop the onions, mushroom stems and the garlic in it. Now, take the mixture to a pan and fry it until they are brown in color. When fried, remove from the pan and set aside. Now, stir the breadcrumbs, parsley, salt and pepper in it. Then the mushrooms are to be filled with the stuffing and sprinkle some vegetable oil over them and then put it in the oven for about 20 minutes. When the mushrooms are lightly browned in color, the stuffed mushrooms are ready to serve. Enjoy!

Vegan queso bean dip

This vegan recipe of dip is very delicious and can be enjoyed with raw vegetables or baked vegetables.

Ingredients
½ cup of refried beans
½ cup of salsa, whichever you prefer

1 cup of vegan sour cream

Method
The beans and the salsa are to be placed in a microwave safe bowl and are to be microwaved until they are warm. Then pour the vegan sour cream to it and stir well. More beans, salsa or cream can be added according to your preference. When the dip is ready, serve them with bread or raw vegetables. Enjoy!

Miso mustard glazed Brussels sprouts

Ingredients
A bag of shaved Brussels sprouts
½ cup of hot water
2 tablespoon of mellow red miso
Dijon mustard

2 cloves of garlic
Arrowroot, 2 teaspoon
Salt and black pepper, to taste

Method
The oven is to be preheated to 400 F. Then the Brussels sprouts are to be placed in a baking dish and set it at a side. Now, take a pot and dissolve the miso in the hot water and then add all the remaining ingredients to it and mix them well. When they are well mixed, pour the mix over the Brussels sprouts and coat them thoroughly. Then the baking dish is to be covered and placed in the preheated oven for about 20 minutes. When tender, the dish is ready to be served. Enjoy!

Chocolate avocado pie

This amazingly delicious to taste dessert is very much liked by the kids and even enjoyed by others fond of sweet dishes and chocolate.

Ingredients
About 2 cups of pecans

4-6 dates

1 tablespoon of maple syrup
2 tablespoon of cocoa powder
1 tablespoon of cinnamon
A pinch Nutmeg, freshly ground
A few drops Vanilla essence
A pinch Sea salt, dried

For filling
Few drops Vanilla essence
2 tablespoons Lemon juice
2-3 avocados
1 can of sweet vegan chocolate chips

Method

For the preparation of crust, pecans are to be soaked in water for at least 3-4 hours. When soaked, drain them. Now, place the pecans in a food processor and chop the dried pecans finely and set aside. Then the dates are to be cut and if they are dry soak them in water. Then add, the dates, maple syrup, cocoa, cinnamon, nutmeg, vanilla and sea salt, to the pecans and blend them until they form a wet mixture. Then, the dough is to be pressed to a pie plate. For preparing the filling, add the ingredients used for filling in a blender. Melt the chocolate chips and cool them. Then the melted chocolate is to be added to the avocado mix and blend it until smooth. Add this mixture over the prepared crust and keep in the refrigerator to chill overnight. Enjoy!

CHOCOLATE PEANUT BUTTER SILKEN PIE

This delicious to taste dessert will definitely be loved by everyone.

Ingredients

4 squares of bakers chocolate, unsweetened
1 cup of peanut butter
1 can of about 16 ounce of silken tofu
1 cup of vegan sugar

Soy milk
1 cup Flour
½ cup of shortening
Water

Method

Mix the flour with salt and cut the vegetable shortening with a fork. Then add water and mix to get a flakier crust. Then roll the dough over a plastic wrap and then poke holes over the dough and bake it until golden brown in color. To prepare the filling, the chocolate is to be melted and then the tofu, peanut butter, and the vegan sugar are to be blended by adding the soy milk to it. Then pour this mixture over the crust and refrigerate it. Enjoy!

IRISH CAPPUCCINO

This beverage is delicious and will be loved by the coffee and chocolate lovers.

Ingredients

4-5 ounces of espresso
Vanilla soymilk
Whiskey

Chocolate flavored syrup

Method

The soymilk is to be steamed and then the espresso is to be added to it. Gently stir the drink and add the whiskey to it and stir it again gently. When mixed top the drink with the chocolate flavored syrup serve. Enjoy!

*I*CE BERRY SHAKE

This delicious smoothie is very easy to prepare and is liked by everyone, especially kids.

Ingredients

A banana, sliced
1 cup of ice cubes
½ cup of berries, frozen

Sweetener, to taste
1 cup of soy milk
1 cup of apple juice

Method

Take a blender, and blend the ice cubes with the sliced bananas, frozen berries, sweetener, and soymilk and apple juice. When the desired creamy consistency of the shake is acheived, serve it. Enjoy!

*C*OCOA-*V*EGGIE SMOOTHIE

This smoothie has a surprising element in it and will definitely be loved by all.

Ingredients

1 Cucumber, sliced
1 Ripe banana, sliced
2 tablespoons Cocoa powder, unsweetened

3-4 fresh mint leaves
Water

Method

Take a blender and pour water into it and then add the banana, cucumber and mint to it and blend them thoroughly. Then the cocoa powder is to be added and blend it again until thoroughly mixed. When the correct texture is formed, serve it. Enjoy!

*H*ASSEL BACK POTATOES

Ingredients

4 medium sized potatoes, peeled
Vegan butter
Olive oil
Fresh thyme leaves
A clove of garlic

Kosher salt and pepper, to taste

Method

The oven is to be preheated to 425 F and line a baking dish with aluminum foil. Then the potatoes are to be sliced lengthwise. Now the butter, oil, thyme, garlic, salt, pepper are to be stirred in a bowl and then coat the potatoes in the mixture. After coating the potatoes thoroughly, place it on the baking sheet and roast it and this can take up to an hour. When baked, serve with your favorite dipping sauce. The sauce can also be made by stirring the yogurt and scallions with a pinch of salt and pepper. Enjoy!

FIVE-VEG LASAGNA

Ingredients

Olive oil
An aborigine, sliced to chunks
15 Mushrooms, chopped
2 Red peppers, chopped and roasted
Lasagna sheets, 8-10

1 can of frozen spinach, defrosted
A 250gm tube of ricotta
Parmesan style cheese, grated
Pine nuts

Method

The oven is to be preheated to 180 C. The olive oil is to be taken to a pan and fry the aborigine in it for about 5 minutes. When softened, transfer it to a bowl and then in the remaining oil, fry the mushrooms until golden brown in color. Then mix the fried mushrooms and peppers in the bowl of aborigine. Now, layer the lasagna sheets and vegetable mixture. Mix the drained spinach, ricotta and half the parmesan cheese together and spoon it over the top layer and then sprinkle the remaining cheese and pine nut over the layer and cover it with foil and bake them in the oven for about 20 minutes. When crispy, serve the delicious dish with salad. Enjoy!

LEMON POSSETS WITH SUGARED-ALMONDS SHORTBREAD

Ingredients

1 cup Double cream
4 tablespoons Golden caster sugar
1 tablespoon Lemon zest
For the shortbread
1 stick Cold butter

1 cup Plain flour
4 tablespoons Golden caster sugar
½ cup Ground rice
½ cup Flaked almonds

Method

The possets are to be made first. To prepare, take a pan and put the cream and sugar to it and heat it gently until the sugar melts. Turn the heat off and then add the lemon zest to it with the lemon juice and let it cool for at least 3 hours. To prepare the shortbread, the oven is to be preheated to 160C and mix the butter and flour in it in a food processor. Then transfer it to a bowl and mix it with the rest of the ingredients that are needed to prepare the shortbread and prepare dough and then bake it in the oven for about 25 minutes. When it turns its color to pale golden, cool it and then cut the shortbread to shards and serve with the possets. Enjoy!

$\mathcal{E}$TON MESS STACKS

This delicious to taste dessert is easy to cook and is enjoyed by everyone.

Ingredients

Whipping Cream 1 cup
Icing sugar, 350gm
Cardamom seeds, crushed
Oil, for greasing

A pot of double cream
½ lemon, juice
Raspberries, 250gm

Method

The whipping cream is to be whisked with the icing sugar until soft peaks form. Add the cardamom and make a firm icing. Fill in a piping bag and pipe onto a greased baking dish and microwave it for about few seconds. Then the cream is to be whipped properly with the lemon juice and then carefully fold the crushed raspberries to the mixture of cream. Place one microwaved cream disc in a glass and serve topped with the cream mixture. Enjoy!

$\mathcal{L}$EMON CURD

Ingredients

A jar of lemon curd
A 500gm tub of Greek yogurt
Raspberries

Icing sugar
Shortbread, used for serving

Method

Take a bowl and add the lemon curd and Greek yogurt to it and fold them for a rippled effect. Then this mixture is to be divided among glasses and the refrigerate it. At the meantime, the raspberries and the icing sugar is to be mixed together and then gently crush it. When the lemon yoghurt mixture is chilled, spoon the raspberry mix over the mixture in the glass and serve it with shortbreads. Enjoy!

$\mathcal{L}$EMON SYLLABUB

Ingredients

1 cup Whipping cream
4 tablespoons Caster sugar
Dash of White wine
Lemon juice and zest of 1 lemon

Berries, to serve

Method

The cream is to be whipped with the sugar until it forms soft peaks. Stir in the wine with it and then pour most of the zest and juice to it and then spoon it in glasses and then sprinkle the rest of the juice and zest and then serve topped with berries. Enjoy!

MELTING-MIDDLE ABORIGINE PARCELS

This is a recipe of meat-free barbeque which can be served with pesto sauce and is very delicious to taste.

Ingredients

3-4 Aborigines
Olive oil
4 Mozzarella balls drained and cut in slices
1 Tomato, sliced in thick pieces
7-8 leaves of basil

For pesto sauce
Basil leaves
Pine nuts
Cloves of garlic
Parmesan style cheese, grated
Olive oil

Method

The pesto sauce is to be prepared first, therefore take all the ingredients of dressing except the olive oil to a food processor and process them gradually by sprinkling olive oil in to it. When processed, transfer it to a bowl.

Now the edges of the aborigines are to be trimmed and move them to a side and then cut the aborigines in slices. Take a barbeque and place the sliced aborigine over it and spread a little olive oil on it and grill it. Now make stacks of Mozzarella, tomato and basil leaves and wrap it in the grilled aborigines and secure it with a cocktail stick. This is to be repeated for all the prepared stacks and is to be kept in refrigerator, overnight. Then the prepared parcels are to be grilled over barbeque, when grilled, serve by sprinkling the pesto sauce over it. Enjoy!

COURGETTE AND HALLOUMI SKEWERS

Ingredients

½ teaspoon of chili powder
1 teaspoon Mint leaves, finely chopped
Lemon zest and juice of 1 lemon

2 courgettes
A packet of 225gm of halloumi cheese, sliced in to cubes

Method

The chili powder, mint, lemon zest and juice, courgettes and halloumi are to be mixed properly. When properly mixed, keep it aside to rest for about 30 minutes. Then the skewers are to be soaked in the mixture for about 20 minutes. The courgettes and the halloumi are to be threaded on the skewers and then the skewers are to be cooked on barbeque for about 8 minutes. When grilled, serve them with the remaining mixture. Enjoy!

NEW POTATO AND TAMARIND SALAD

In India, tamarind is widely used for flavoring potatoes and also used for preparing low fat and delicious salads.

Ingredients

About 2 tablespoons of tamarind paste
Muscovado sugar
2 teaspoons Cumin, ground

1 kg potatoes
1 tablespoon Low fat yogurt
1 tablespoon cilantro, chopped

Method

To prepare the dressing of the dish, the tamarind pulp is to be taken in a bowl and add boiling water with sugar, cumin, and ginger to it. Bring the mixture to boil and let it simmer, until the mixture thickens. In the meantime, take another large sized bowl and pour water and salt to it and bring it to boil and then the potatoes are to be added to it and are to be cooked, until the potatoes soften, this can take about 10-15 minutes. When the potatoes are tender, drain and peel them. Transfer the potatoes to the bowl with the dressing and coat the potatoes well with the mix. Serve the dish by sprinkling yogurt and coriander over it. Enjoy!

INDIAN STYLE TIKKA SKEWERS

This delicious to taste dish is easy to cook and is flavored like Indian-style kebabs.

Ingredients

3 tablespoon of tikka paste (you will find this in any Indian store in your locality)
A 500gm tub of yogurt
1 teaspoon Cumin seeds
1Ginger, grated
1 10 oz. packet of Cottage cheese, sliced
250gm potatoes

2-3 Red onions, peeled and cut in to wedges
Mango pickle, to serve
Leaves of mint, for garnish
A bag of salad leaves, for garnish
12 Flat Breads

Method

The bamboo skewers are to be soaked in water for about 30 minutes. Take a large bowl, mix the tikka paste, half the yogurt, cumin, ginger and mix well. The potatoes are to be cooked in boiling salted water over low heat for about 8 minutes. Then, the potatoes are to be drained and coated in the curry paste mixture with the cottage cheese and keep it aside for at least 2 hours. Then the kebabs are to be arranged and are to be threaded with the potatoes, cottage cheese on the skewer with onions and pepper and grill it over the barbeque. Take the mango pickle, rest of the yogurt, mint leaves and barbeque it for 15 minutes. Then the chapattis are to be added to the barbeque and grill it again. Then the barbequed skewers are ready to be served with the side of the mint salad, mango pickle, yogurt and chapattis. Enjoy!

TOMATO, CUCUMBER & CILANTRO SALAD

Ingredients

2 Vine tomatoes, chopped
1 small sized cucumber

1 red onion, sliced
6 tablespoon of fresh, chopped corianders

Method

The ingredients used in the salad, deseeded and chopped tomatoes, cucumber, onion, and corianders are to be mixed properly in a bowl. The only way to prepare a good salad is to mix the ingredients in a correct proportion. When the ingredients are mixed properly, chill for an hour and serve it immediately. Enjoy!

SKINNY CARROT FRIES

This delicious to taste dish is loved by kids and is at the same time very healthy, won't be a problem if the kids gorge on it for evening snacks.

Ingredients

A few tablespoons Olive oil
2 big Carrots
1 tablespoon of corn flour

1 bunch Tarragon, chopped
Black pepper

Method

The oven is to be preheated to 200 C and a baking dish is to be lined. The carrots are to be cut in thin slices and coat them with corn flour and pepper. The oil is to be tossed with it and then place them on the baking dish and cook them in the oven for about 45 minutes. When the carrots are fried, serve them by mixing salt and tarragon over the fries. Enjoy!

STUFFED JACKET POTATOES

Ingredients

4-5 Medium sized potatoes
1 cup Cheddar cheese, grated
100 grams Sweet corn

½ cup Mixed peppers, diced
Fresh herbs like that of thymes, basil or coriander

Method

The oven is to be preheated to 200 C and the baking dish is to be lined, then the potatoes are to be baked for about an hour until the skin of the potatoes are crispy and then set them aside. The potatoes are now to be cut into halves and spoon out the middle of the potato and repeat it with all the halves. Then the scooped out potatoes are to be placed in a bowl and mashed adding cheese, peppers and sweet corns. Then mix it well and after mixing them well, spoon the stuff back to the skin of the potato and place it on the baking dish and bake it until it in golden in color. Serve when cooked. Enjoy!

*P*ITA POCKET

Ingredients

A whole-meal pita bread
4 tablespoons Humus

Watercress, spinach and rocket salad mix
Olive oil

Method

The pita bread is to be halved forming two pockets and toast it until brown and crispy. Pour the humus inside the halves and spoon the salad in it, sprinkling the oil over it and then tuck it. The pitta pocket is ready to be served. Enjoy!

*C*HEESY VEG BURGERS

Ingredients

2 tablespoons Olive oil
2 leeks
200 grams Mushrooms
2 Carrots, peeled and chopped
1 tablespoon of seasoning
2 tablespoons Soy sauce

1 can of beans
½ cup Cheddar cheese, grated
4 slices of granary bread, torn in pieces
Burger bun
Lettuce
Tomatoes

Method

Some oil is to be heated in a pan over medium heat and then the vegetables are to be added, with the seasoning and soy sauce and cooked for about 10minutes. When the vegetables soften, add them to the food processor with beans, cheese, and bread and process it until a thick paste is formed. Now, the paste is to be shaped in form of burger patty, keep it in the refrigerator to get chill. Then, take some oil in a pan and fry each sides of the burger patty for about 3minutes, until they are crispy. Serve it with the buns and salad, ketchup and mayonnaise. Enjoy!

*H*OMEMADE *C*AJUN TORTILLAS

Ingredients

2 tablespoons Oil
1 tablespoon Cajun spice mix

8 Plain tortillas

Method

The oven is to be preheated to 80 degrees C. Mix the Cajun spice mix with the oil and brush it over the tortillas. The stacks are them one over the other and cut in wedges. Place them on baking dish and bake it until the color turns golden. When crispy, serve it. Enjoy!

Marinated feta in thyme and chili oil

Ingredients

3 tablespoons Olive oil
Fresh leaves of thyme
4 Cloves of garlic, chopped
1 teaspoon Chili flakes

A pack of artichoke hearts in oil
Two packets of feta cheese
16 Kalamata olives

Method

Add the olive oil and thyme to a bowl and then blend it with a hand blender. Stir in the chili, garlic and black peppers and mix well. Slice the feta cheese and arrange it in a dish with the tomatoes, artichokes and olives. Spoon the prepared oil on to the cheese, artichokes and leave them to marinate overnight. The dish is ready to be served. Enjoy!

Cheesecake Ice Cream

Ingredients

¾ cup Cashews
1 cup Vegan cream cheese
½ cup Soy milk
1 cup Sugar

3 tablespoons Lemon juice
Few drops of Vanilla essence
A pinch of Salt

Method

The cashews should be powdered in a food processor. Then the grounded cashews, cream. Sugar, lemon juice, vanilla essence and salt are to be blended in a blender, until smooth. Then keep the smooth mix in the refrigerator for at least 2-3 hours. Turn on the ice cream maker and leave it on overnight add the mixture and freeze the ice cream as per the instructions on your machine.. Process until light and creamy and serve immediately! Enjoy!

Carrots and nothing else cake

This is a vegetarian cake without the use of eggs, that is very delicious to taste and easy to make.

Ingredients

½ cup canola oil
5 tablespoons Apple sauce
2 tablespoons Egg replacer
2 cups Sugar
About 3 cups of carrots, shredded
A pinch of Salt

1 teaspoon Baking soda
2 teaspoons Pie spice

Method

The oven is to be preheated to 350 C. Now all the wet ingredients like that of oil, apple sauce, and egg replacer should be mixed well with sugar and then the shredded carrots need to add to it and mix them well. Now, take another bowl and mix the dry ingredients and when mixed properly, both the dry and wet ingredients are to be mixed well to form a batter. Then pour the batter into the cake pan and bake it in the oven for about 40-45 minutes. When baked, let the cake cool and serve. Enjoy!

AVOCADO HUMMUS

This recipe of a dip is very delicious and easy to prepare. The dip can be enjoyed with raw and baked vegetables, vegan crackers, sandwich and fennel.

Ingredients

A tin of chickpeas
2-3 cloves of garlic
Lemon juice
2 tablespoon of tahini

Avocado, 2
Salt
Paprika

Method

Add the chickpeas, garlic, lemon juice and the tahini to a blender and blend them until smooth, if required some water can also be added. Now, add the avocados and blend again, season to taste and then pour it to a bowl and serve after sprinkling paprika over it. Enjoy!

HERBED WHITE BEAN DIP

This recipe of dip is easy to prepare and can be enjoyed with baked and raw vegetables alike.

Ingredients

Parsley leaves, chopped
Leaves of basil
Cloves of garlic
A small sized shallots, chopped

1 can of white kidney beams
Lemon juice
Cayenne pepper
Pepper, ground

Method

Place all the ingredients in a food processor, except the salt and pepper and blend well, until they are smooth. When well blended, transfer it to a bowl and season to taste and then serve it by garnishing it with basil leaves. Enjoy!

GRILLED PORTOBELLO BURGER WITH ONION JAM

Ingredients

2 pounds thinly sliced large red onions
⅔ cup low-fat plain yogurt
3 tablespoons prepared horseradish
4 tablespoons extra-virgin olive oil
4 split and toasted whole grain buns or whole wheat English muffins
2 sprigs fresh thyme
1 cup red wine

Salt and black pepper
¼ cup honey
¼ cup red wine vinegar
1 garlic clove, crushed
2 tablespoons balsamic vinegar
1 pound stemmed large Portobello mushrooms
Lettuce leaves

Method

Discard water from the yogurt by hanging it in a cheese cloth for an hour. Now, heat 2 tablespoon olive oil in a skillet and add the onions, salt and pepper as per the taste and cover and cook for 15 minutes. Add the red wine to it and cook with high heat. Add the red-wine vinegar and honey and cook it till the onions get a thick jam-like texture. In a different preheated pan, add rest of the olive-oil with vinegar. Now add lettuce leaves and sprigs of thyme. Coat the mushrooms and grill it with olive-oil for 3-4 minutes, make the sandwich with the mushrooms, onion jam, lettuce and buns. Serve it fresh. Enjoy!

GRILLED SWEET POTATOES WITH CILANTRO AND LIME

Ingredients

3 sweet potatoes
Freshly ground pepper
2 teaspoons zest of finely grated lime
Pinch of pepper

¼ cup canola oil
¼ cup finely chopped fresh cilantro
Kosher salt

Method

Boil the potatoes in water till tender. Cool them down and slice them, but do not mash them up. Preheat the grill on a medium heat. In a bowl mix the cayenne pepper with salt and lime zest. Now, brush the potato slices with the peeper salt mixture and cook it for 1 to ½ minutes on the preheated grill. Season the baked potatoes with salt and cilantro mixture. Serve it warm and fresh. Enjoy!

SMOKY CORN ON THE COB

Ingredients

2 Corn cobs
4 tablespoons Butter

Salt to taste
Paprika to taste

Method

Wash the corns carefully but do not pill it from the husks as the whole thing is needed for this preparation. Peel back the husks from the corn and remove the silk neatly. Butter the kernels thoroughly and add the salt on it as per the taste. Now, add the smoked paprika. Fold back the husks again on the corn and place it in grill. Cook it on low heat for ten to fifteen minutes. Turn the corns to bake it properly. Serve it warm. Enjoy!

Grilled Ratatouille Salad

Ingredients

3 medium tomatoes
1 medium zucchini
½ cup fresh basil leaves
3 tablespoons extra-virgin olive oil
1 small eggplant
Kosher salt

1 medium red bell pepper
1 small red onion
Freshly ground pepper
1 tablespoon and 2 teaspoons red wine vinegar

Method

Slice the basil leaves thinly and wash it properly. Slice the eggplant in thick rounds and soak it in salted water for up to 20 minutes. Now, slice the zucchini and tomato in round shapes. Put the olive oil on the vegetables by brushing them and marinade them for a while. Add some salt on them and put them on a preheated grill. Grill the vegetables until they get soft. Add vinegar on it and now set the cooked item in plate in a circular way serve them hot. Enjoy!

Two-Bean Chili for weeknights

Ingredients

¼ teaspoon Chinese five-spice powder
1 ¼ cups low-sodium vegetable
1 tablespoon vegetable oil
1 minced small jalapeno
1 small or ½ large red onion
2 teaspoons red wine vinegar
1 large clove garlic, minced
½ cup Cheddar extra-sharp and finely shredded

1 cup crushed and canned roasted tomatoes
1 and ½ tablespoons chili powder
Two 15-ounce cans of rinsed and drained beans
2 tablespoons chopped fresh cilantro
2 cups cooked brown rice

Method

Add the jalapenos in a medium heated sauce pan with oil. Now, add the vinegar and onions in it. Cook it for five minutes and add the garlic cook it for half a minute more. Add the tomatoes, chili powder and other spice powders in it. Place the sauce pan on high heat and cook the mixture well. Add the beans and boil them. Now, reduce the heat and heat until thickened. Add the cilantro in it and serve immediately in bowls after sprinkle the cheddar. Enjoy!

SPICY VEGAN SLOPPY JOES

It is a spicy dish which is best served at diner. This recipe is very easy to cook and also fun to serve.

Ingredients

1 small de-seeded and diced green bell pepper
Shredded red cabbage or lettuce
3 tablespoons tomato paste
1 pound cremini mushrooms, halved
1 tablespoon extra-virgin olive oil
1 large sweet onion, diced

1 ¾ cups light beer
Kosher salt
⅓ cup finely chopped walnuts
Freshly ground black pepper
¼ cup ketchup
6 whole grain hamburger buns
½ teaspoon chipotle chili powder

Method

Chop the mushrooms first, now take a large non sticky pan and heat the same with oil in it. Add the onions with one tablespoon beer and a little salt on the saucepan. Cook the same well for 5 minutes. Now add the pepper and walnuts in it and cook for more 3 minutes. Now, add the chopped mushroom and chipotle powder with ¾ teaspoon of black pepper let it cook for 5 more minutes. Add the rest of the ingredients and cook it well now. Serve the same after spooning the mixture in the bun. Enjoy!

LENTIL SOUP

Ingredients

½ teaspoon coriander
½ cup finely chopped carrot
2 tablespoons olive oil
½ cup finely chopped celery
2 teaspoons kosher salt
1 pound picked and rinsed lentils

2 quarts vegetable broth
½ teaspoon toasted cumin
½ teaspoon grains of paradise
1 cup finely chopped onion
1 cup peeled and chopped tomatoes

Method

Heat the olive oil at a medium temperature and add the onion when it is hot. Now, add the celery, carrot and salt in it and cook it well for six to seven minutes. After that add the tomatoes, broth, coriander and all the other ingredients and cook it for thirty to forty minutes at high heat. Cool it a little and serve it warm. Enjoy!

VEGETARIAN RIBOLLITA

This soup is famous for the moth watering taste.

Ingredients

½ cup shaved Pecorino-Romano
¼ cup extra-virgin olive oil
1 medium onion, diced (2 ½ cups)
10 cups vegetable broth
1 rib celery, sliced (¾ cups)
1 medium zucchini, diced (1 ¼ cups or 5 ¼ ounces)
2 carrots, peeled and diced (⅓ cup)
3 cloves garlic, chopped
Fresh rosemary 1 sprig
Kosher salt

Freshly ground black pepper
1 coarsely chopped head Savoy cabbage
1 (15-ounce) can tomatoes cut it in diced shape
½ cup chopped fresh basil leaves
1 teaspoon dried marjoram
4 cups cubed sourdough bread (about ½ loaf)
3 cups baby spinach leaves
1 (15-ounce) can cannellini beans

Method

Heat the olive oil on medium heat and add all the ingredients, when the oil gets hot except the cabbage, tomatoes, marjoram and basil. Cook it well for ten to fifteen minutes until the vegetables get softer. Now add the rest of the vegetables and add salt as per the taste. Cook it for more ten minutes. Stir the beans and place the pot on a low heat for more twenty minutes. Now remove the rosemary spring. Stir the spinach and bread. Now place the soup on high heat to gain the thickness and serve warm when with a cheese garnish. Enjoy!

SALAD WITH ROASTED BUTTERNUT AND TANGERINE-ROSEMARY VINAIGRETTE

This is a recipe which contains a lot of carbohydrates and is an energy booster.

Ingredients

6 cups loosely packed and fresh spinach
4 cups of ½ pounds of peeled and seeded butternut squash
3 teaspoons fresh rosemary roughly chopped

4 tangerines
¼ cup dried cranberries
4 tablespoons extra-virgin olive oil
Salt and freshly ground pepper

Method

Toss the squash with olive oil and season it with rosemary, salt and pepper. Roast it in a preheated oven at 400 degrees F for twenty minutes. Now cool it down for fifteen minutes. Slice 3 tangerines and squeeze the juice from the remaining one. Add salt and rosemary in it and season it well. Now combine the squash, tangerines and cranberries and toss it. Place it in the salad plate and serve. Enjoy!

Curried Butternut Squash Soup

Ingredients

1 teaspoon curry powder
2 cups vegetable broth
1 teaspoon garlic powder
1 teaspoon onion powder

Lime zest
Lime Cream
Salt and ground black pepper
2 halves butternut squash roasted

Method

Place the butternut squash in a saucepan and heat on a medium heat. Now add the garlic powder, curry powder, broth in it. Now add salt and pepper as per the taste. Let the pot heat over medium heat for a while. Puree the soup by blending it. Put it in the soup bowl and serve it with lime cream. To prepare the lime cream use ½ cup sour cream, ¼ teaspoon lime zest and 1 table spoon lime zest. Combine the total and the cream is ready to use. Enjoy!

Classic Macaroni and Cheese Recipe

Ingredients

4 cups whole milk
8 tablespoons of unsalted butter
½ cup of all-purpose flour
kosher salt

elbow macaroni
224 grams sharp cheddar cheese
84 pecorino romano cheese
⅔ cup of poncho

Method

Heat the milk over simmer heat and in a huge heavy pan, liquefy the butter over simmer. Add the flour and keep whisking until it turns light brown in color Gradually add the hot milk to the mixture until smooth and combined. Mix 1 tablespoon of the salt and remove it and set aside. Add the pasta and persist cooking, moving constantly, until the pasta is warmed through and steaming, takes about 4 minutes. Serve without delay. Enjoy!

Classic Peach Pie

Ingredients

1 pie bread
4 lbs. peaches
½ cup of sugar
¼ cup of corn starch
1 lime
large pinch of salt beaten

Method

Adjust the oven at 425° F. In a huge bowl, combine, sugar, peach slices, cornstarch and lime zest. Flip the mixture until the peaches are consistently coated, then decant into the ready, chilled pie shell. Place the fruit in the chilled crown crust, shape as required. Chill the bent pie for at least 20 minutes. Shower with sugar and heat at 425° for 15 minutes. After 15 minutes, lower the furnace heat to 375°. Bake until the top is golden brown the filling is bubbling all over. Serve without delay. Enjoy!

CLASSIC BAKED MACARONI AND CHEESE

Ingredients

225 grams elbow macaroni
2 tablespoon butter
2 tablespoon all-purpose flour
2 cups of milk

½ tablespoon salt
½ tablespoon ground black pepper
¼ tablespoon red pepper
225 grams sharp cheddar cheese

Method

Dissolve butter in a large Dutch or saucepan furnace over simmer heat. Beat in flour until smooth. Beat constantly 2 minutes, slowly beat in milk, and cook, whisk constantly for 5 minutes. Remove from heat, mix in salt, black pepper, add 1 cup of shredded cheese, and ripe pasta. Spoon pasta combination into an evenly greased 2 qt. baking bowl; cover with remaining 1 cup of cheese and heat at 400° for 20 minutes. Let stand 10 minutes before serving. Serve without delay. Enjoy!

CLASSIC AMERICAN APPLE PIE

Ingredients

2½ cups of flour
ice water
2 sticks of butter
1 tablespoon sugar
1 tablespoon salt

2 apples
½ cup of brown sugar
2 tablespoon flour
1 tablespoon cinnamon

Method

To make the pastry, we need to beat the flour, salt mutually in a huge basin and the ice water and mix with your fingers until the bread comes together as one in a ball. Refrigerate for at least 30min. Adjust furnace at 375 F degrees and shower some flour on work station. Roll out one of the pieces of pastry into a round that's huge enough for an 8 inch pie plate. Shift the pastry onto the pie dish and include the apple mix to the bottom crust and cautiously place over the top of the pie. Bake until golden. Serve without delay. Enjoy!

Classic American Fare, Now In Vegan!

Ingredients

¼ cup of vegan butter
1 cup onion
½ tablespoon garlic
450 grams broccoli
¼ tablespoon white pepper

Corn starch
½ cup of water
¼ cup of nutritional yeast
1½ cups soy milk
250 grams vegan cheddar cheese

Method

In an average sized saucepan over simmer high heat, liquefy 2 tablespoons vegan butter and garlic, sauté onion and broccolis stems and include milk, salt, yeast, cheese, and water then remove them from heat. In an average skillet over simmer heat, heat residual butter, add broccoli florets, and fry until turned bright green. Remove them from the flame and include broccoli to soup pot. Combine and season with pepper and more salt to flavor. Add corn starch to make it thicker. Serve without delay. Enjoy!

CONCLUSION

The book has been written for those people who are not only health conscious, but also for those people who want to prepare exciting vegetarian dishes. Veggies are not only full of roughage and fibers, but also help in maintaining a complete balanced diet. The ingredients in the book are written perfectly with the tips and their actual quantity. The best thing about the book is that I have made sure that I have used the most cheaply available products in the market. Each and every ingredient can be gathered from the market, and I have also shown my different experiment with texture and taste. In the book we also find that vegetarian dishes not only include the main courses, but also deserts and sweets. The dishes gives you a fine dining experience and even make you have a healthy diet control.

Thank you again for purchasing this book!

Finally, if you enjoyed this book, please take the time to share your thoughts and post a review on Amazon. It'd be greatly appreciated!

Feel free to contact me at emma.katie@outlook.com

Check out more books by Emma Katie at:

www.amazon.com/author/emmakatie

Made in the USA
Middletown, DE
20 May 2017